[THE WRITING BOOK]

All about writing:
from Business Proposals
to Press Releases
to Prose and Poetry

By
Joe Marconi

*"You can write about anything, and if you write well enough,
even the reader with no intrinsic interest in the subject
will become involved."*
— Tracy Kidder

*"It's not wise to violate the rules
until you know how to observe them."*
— T.S. Eliot

[The Writing Book]

ISBN-10: 0-9819095-0-7

ISBN-13: 978-0-9819095-0-9

Cover Design: Gregory S. Paus

Published by

**Dickens~Webster
Publishing**

A division of
Bruce Bendinger Creative Communications, Inc.

• 2144 N. Hudson • Chicago, IL 60614 •
• TEL: 773-871-1179 • FAX: 773-281-4643 •
dickenswebster@gmail.com

**Dickens~Webster
Publishing**

This book is, as always,
for Todd and Kristin and Emily, and for Karin.

It is also for the writers and other very smart people who taught
me about writing and caused me to love books and the written
word, and for my students, from whom I continue to learn.

And for the usual suspects,
Rich Girod, Lonny Bernardi, Guy Kendler, and editor/publisher/
raconteur/bon vivant and friend Bruce Bendinger.

Contents

Part Two: Topics

Words are the most powerful drug used by mankind.
— **Rudyard Kipling**

My aim is to put down what I see and what I feel
in the best and simplest way I can tell it.
— **Ernest Hemingway**

Writing is the only thing that ... when I'm doing it, I don't feel
that I should be doing something else instead.
— **Gloria Steinem**

I wrote from a sense of need. I needed something to do.
You can't just sleep all day long.
— **Snoopy, writing in** *Snoopy's Guide to the Writing Life*

The difference between the almost right word and the right word
is really a large matter – it's the difference between
the lightning bug and the lightning.
— **Mark Twain**

Why Good Writing Matters

My task... is, by the power of the written word to make you hear,
to make you feel – it is, before all, to make you see.
That – and no more – and it is everything.
                                          — Joseph Conrad

Yet another book about writing? Well… yes.

"What makes this one different?" That's a fair question.

The short answer is that I wrote this one, and it represents what I think is the best way to get yourself to the next level as a writer.

Now, here's the long answer.

Amazon.com lists some 530,800 titles under "writing" in its books category. Though there are no truly reliable statistics as to how many books you will probably read in a lifetime, it would be safe to guess it will be a good deal less than 530,800. Even the most learned of writers, myself included, has likely only flipped through a few of those titles.

Some books on writing are predictable, formal textbooks, written in a stiff, no-nonsense style that reduces writing to imperatives – your basic do's and don'ts. Some are how-to books that emphatically list simple-yet-sure-fire steps to becoming a wealthy and famous author.

Then there are the memoirs of some well-known – and many unknown – writers who deliver conversational advice about their craft. With luck, these memoirs are nicely seasoned with interesting stories about running into Papa Hemingway in a bar and trading *bon mots* (that's a French term meaning "witty remarks" – some writers use a lot of French terms that we're all assumed to know).

Some books on writing are boring. Some are entertaining.

As to the question of whether they actually help aspiring writers, the answer is yes... and no.

Some Do: Many Don't.

Whether the person reading this book right now (that's you) is a student in a writing class, an executive looking for help creating more effective written materials for business, someone who aspires to write for fame and fortune, or just a person looking for a guide to creative self-expression, there are no guarantees that this – or any – book will do that. Because, in writing, a lot of it is really up to you. Sometimes it's *all* up to you.

Writing is not rocket science. Kurt Vonnegut compared writing instruction to lessons from a golf pro. A teacher can't make someone a great golfer, but he or she can probably help you shave a few strokes off your game.

Gay Talese had a useful point of view. "The 'best advice' I think is in reading good writers... for we learn best by emulating the best."

There is certainly truth to that. One thing successful writers appear to have in common is that they are also avid readers. And, if we want to read about writing, we have 530,800 more books waiting for us – just as soon as we finish this one.

For me, this book was inevitable. Most published writers are asked routinely how they do it. Where do we get our ideas? How do we overcome fears about writing? How do we overcome writer's block? How do we know if our writing is any good? Is it necessary to outline first? Where is the best place to write? And when? When does research become plagiarism? What about getting published? Is it necessary to have an agent? And so on.

After writing more than a dozen books, editing five more, ghostwriting at least four others, and contributing shorter pieces to more than several books, newspapers, and magazines, it was time to write about writing.

On top of that, there were the invitations to teach a writing class at two colleges. It was time to put what I knew into some sort of organized format – a book.

Every writer gets something out of the writing experience, and we all relate to the process in different ways. What works for Stephen King or Kurt Vonnegut doesn't necessarily help a PR writer shape up a press release, nor does it benefit a reporter writing for a newspaper's business page or a magazine feature writer, a speechwriter, or someone responsible for newsletters or ad copy.

For every type of writing, there are differences and distinctions, rules and tips on organization, and variations in form and style. Looking at writing from many sides and following where the muse (or the editor) leads can be rewarding on many levels personally and professionally.

And, at some point, we have to share that experience – which is probably why there are 530,800 books on writing.

Road Trip

This book is also a road trip. Together, we'll have a series of writing adventures. These adventures won't teach you all there is to know about writing, but they should help you get started with developing the right habits and the right frame of mind. As you'll see, it's not just about learning new things, it's about finding and opening new doors, and developing new habits. It's a journey that may take you to new places where you discover some interesting possibilities.

From Gutenberg's invention of the printing press to today's instant messaging and the ever-expanding blogosphere, the purpose of good writing really hasn't changed all that much. But the rules of writing have changed dramatically. Most importantly, the places where writing is read and the places where it's needed have changed a great deal – and that will be a big part of our writing road trip.

A Variety of Audiences

The Writing Book is an introduction to writing for a variety of audiences. It's about writing for specific audiences through direct written communication and it's about appealing to the general public through the mass media. We'll journey through all the different forms of writing in the 20th... no, make that the 21st Century.

Chapter by chapter, you'll receive an overview and an introduction to various kinds of writing: for advertising and public relations, news reporting, creative nonfiction, fiction, biography, and many other commercial applications of the written word... like speechwriting. We'll cover the basic forms and formats of each of these genres – print and broadcast copy, brochures, direct mail, press releases, formal and informal speeches, and Internet communications. And, if you want to go further down the path, we'll provide you with some next steps on your journey.

In each chapter, the objective will be pretty much the same – to provide a solid basis for continuing on, if you desire, to more advanced levels of writing for that specific field or discipline.

Writing for the Ear. Writing for the Eye.

From a child's first block letters to the words on the teleprompter for the evening TV news, writing is, at its very least, about communicating. Writing "for public communication" can be about writing for publication or providing the information or material from which others will communicate with the public.

We may read the words. Or, we may hear them.

This is a big thought. Think about it for a minute. Even that simple difference can be profound.

OK, here is another big thought. The actual word "communication" comes from the Latin word *communicare*, meaning to impart or to share. Whether the communicator is sharing objective information or a subjective expression of sentiment, we need to "get it right" as it moves from the writer to the reader. The price of getting it wrong is high. It can create misunderstanding, hurt, and destruction. In terms of what we share, the admonition to "write it down" has potential life-and-death implications.

And that is the final big thought. Write it right. The written word is the simplest, most efficient and potentially the most powerful form of communication and it stays with us long after the room, theater stage, the screen, or television is silent.

> *Through the eyes of the writer, readers examine life –*
> *history, the present, and the future. The best writers let us see*
> *through binoculars that magnify and enrich experience;*
> *they allow us to see with broader, deeper insight.*
> — **Helena Hjalmarrson**

A Critical Question

Next big question: Is what you're writing, even in a small way, worth writing about? Every writer has to ask this critical question. Will someone somehow be better for receiving the information provided in what I have written?

Whether the subject of the written work is a person, a product, a company, an event, a story, a weight-loss plan, a gallon of gasoline or the earth itself, information – whether presented to educate or to entertain – should be presented in such a way that it is interesting and have content value. A book, a pamphlet, a newspaper, a magazine, an ad, a press release, white paper, a fact book, a script, a package label, notes on a CD jewel box, a Web site or blog, or a medicine bottle should convey its message in an interesting and informative manner.

Whether aesthetic or practical, *what you write must have value.* The consumer of the information depends on it. Careers and businesses depend on it. Writing matters.

Introduce Yourself to the Writer Inside
The best introduction to writing often begins inside ourselves.

It can start with the introduction to you – particularly as you work to discover the writer inside. Ask yourself these simple, but profound, questions. Write them down if you'd like. Short answers are fine. And there is a very important target audience – you.

- Who are you?
- Where did you come from?
- What do you do?
- What have you done?
- What do you want to do?
- What are the three things that matter most to you?
- What would you change about your life, space, or world?
- Why should people care about what you have to say?
- What insight or perspective do you bring to your story?

From answering these questions and then getting the words on paper, the process begins. From there, you can go in any number of directions, elaborating on some points and minimizing or deleting others.

When you're finished, ask yourself what the words you've written might accomplish – what do they say about you, your life, your times? Is there something you've written that is unique or distinctive. How have you made it worth the reader's time? Whatever the answer, how do you feel about that? Are you satisfied or would you like to change it?

After all, great writers also rewrite.

A Simple Assignment
Complete the sentence that begins with the words:

Happiness is…

You'll probably think about quite a few things before you write something you're happy with.

What ends up in your final edited and polished version will be a part of what all writers learn about writing. Whether for business, creativity, to educate or entertain, quite simply, writing starts with the writer. It is an art – one that you can master.

It might lead to a passing grade, a diploma, an advanced degree, a job, a sale, a connection, or an investment in an idea or a business. It might be about an escape to another world, a vision, a funny or fantastic adventure set in motion, or something that surprises even the writer. The tipping point that leads to success may very well be your writing... **because good writing matters.**

Reading: You, Your Readers, & Time

Next to doing things that deserve to be written,
nothing gets a man more credit, or gives him more pleasure
than to write things that deserve to be read.
— **Lord Chesterfield**

Reading and writing are like inhaling and exhaling. They go together. Similarly, one of the first steps on your journey to becoming a writer is to become a better reader.

What have you read recently? A magazine article? A report? A letter? A script? An essay? A poem? A proposal? Minutes of a meeting? An ad? Think about it – each had a different form and format.

Next, consider the subject. If it's a book – a book about what? Finance? Art? Biography? History? Cooking? Fiction? If an article, is it to educate? To entertain? Announce something? Inform? Criticize or review? Respond to criticism? Offer a different perspective on prevailing or conventional opinion?

Form. Format. Content. Objective. As a reader, you need to look behind the curtain. Start to understand the structural components of what you read. More on this later.

Writing, Reading, Form, Substance, Subject… and Style.

Just as different forms of writing have different structures, they also have different styles. What's the appropriate style for whatever you're writing?

Will the words be presented in a breezy, conversational – perhaps even an amusing style? Or will they be hard-hitting? Angry? Provocative? Critical? Understated? Scholarly? Factual? Lyrical?

Stream of consciousness? Romantic? Reflecting a thoughtful insight or depth of knowledge of the subject? In rhyme? Or done to time?

Will the material be offered in a journalistic fashion, focusing on who, what, when, where, why, and perhaps how? Will opinions and conclusions be offered that challenge presumed or established facts? Will it qualify as literature?

As writers, some of us may be able to develop a number of different styles, depending on the project. Others will find their strength (and success) in one kind of writing, and stick to that.

If the work is shorter, such as a pamphlet or a brochure, will the tone be reflective of any of the above descriptions – only shorter? And, will the writer need help?

What help might you need? Perhaps you will interview experts to validate or invalidate a particular premise or point of view? Maybe you will write a "bible." Whether in long or short form, that's what we call a work that is classified as definitive, essential, or "must" reading? Who knows? Some day, that author might be you.

A Good Book on Reading
In 2001, Yale University professor and literary critic Harold Bloom published what proved to be a best-selling book with the unlikely title – in a commercial sense, at least – *How to Read and Why*. Bloom described reading as "the most healing of pleasures." His instructions were that it should be done "slowly, with love, openness, and with our inner ear cocked. Then we should reread, reread, reread, and do so aloud as often as possible." While the inference might be drawn that Bloom is referring to reading books – possibly fiction, perhaps even poetry – the same approach may be taken with a magazine or a newspaper article. Listen to the rhythm of the information in a newspaper article. Then listen to how a good feature writer strings together a longer narrative.

What about business writing? Business writing should have its own rhythm. Even a memo or a business plan, where the author hopes for a major investment, should be interesting and persuasive reading.

Finally, does your writing respect the reader's time? Harold Bloom's well-intentioned advice notwithstanding, who in these fast-paced, stressful days has time to "reread, reread, reread?" Well, the fact is that we do. If we're really serious about becoming better writers. Even though we're all busier than ever these days, if we truly want to train that "inner ear," we need to give ourselves the time to read – and read well.

You Can't Read All of the People All of the Time.

Certainly, the same advice isn't the right advice for everyone all the time. Every reader, consumer, practitioner, and student has different tastes, different interests, different levels of comprehension and appreciation, and certainly different time schedules.

That said, Bloom's basic point is still a good one. And certain clichés seem to apply. For example, If you want something done, give it to someone who is busy. It seems to be true (many clichés are true) that busy people always seem able to "make time." They get more accomplished and seem to get more out of the things they do – including reading.

Conversely, those who complain constantly about never having enough time, seem to have an amazing talent for wasting it, often putting up a great show of breathless activity in the process of accomplishing little. Though they *do* support the economy by purchasing large numbers of clipboards and file folders – and by consulting their Blackberry's often.

Is it simply that some people are better time managers or are more organized?

Whatever the problem, we suggest that a little more reading wouldn't hurt – perhaps one of those self-help books or one more book on writing (as mentioned, there are many to choose from). And, if you like a book, read it again to see if you missed anything the first time. Chances are you did. Better yet, you will better understand what you liked about the writing.

Certainly, Professor Bloom can indulge his passion for reading, rereading, rereading. After all, that is also his job. For those of us who are "average readers," once might be enough for most books and articles. But we can still become better readers.

As you become a better reader, you may discover an additional bonus. Good writers and avid readers seem to be better at doing what they want to do and accomplishing what they want to get done. They have richer, more productive lives. Becoming a good writer (and reader) has more benefits than you may realize.

The Joy of Reading

The essays in this book make frequent references to the joy of reading and a love of books. That is not a universal trait. For some people, reading is a chore. Perhaps they need a Professor Bloom to help teach them how to read and how to enjoy it.

Some people avoid books. Trying to convince people they are missing a great deal is usually a waste of everyone's time, as they tend to be programmed to give an hour of explanation on why they don't have time to read. Save yourself the effort – you can devote that hour to reading.

Reading is great exercise for your mind. It does, in fact, educate and entertain. The result? "A well-furnished mind." The brain does not do well "running on empty."

One more thing, you don't have to finish reading everything you start. It is perfectly okay to begin reading a book or an article and not finish reading it to the very end if it is not providing what you need.

Let's face it, some books or subject matter are not to everyone's taste. In some cases, educators do their students a huge disservice by simply assigning works to be read without first letting the student know why these works have value.

In other cases, it is the writer's fault. After all, even though quality writing is subjective, published writing should be worth reading. Sad to say, not all of it is. And even this offers a lesson. If you decide to stop reading, it might be useful to understand why. Where did this writer lose you as a reader?

So, let us, each in our own way, commit to become better readers. As we do, we will be on the way to also becoming better writers.

When reading…

- **Make yourself comfortable**. Some people get more from reading when they have complete quiet and privacy; others are accustomed to having music playing or ambient conversation in the background. Find a place, a space, and an environment that allows you to focus on what you're reading so you can best enjoy and absorb its content.

- **Keep a note pad and a pen handy**. Most people are likely to come across words, terms, facts, or quotations they either don't understand or want to be sure to remember later. Writing the word or quote on a separate sheet, rather than underlining or highlighting the text, allows you to draw greater attention to it at the time. Reinforce it mentally. Create a reference note to follow up later. This is more effective than interrupting your reading to look up the term or simply skipping over it.

- **Recognize that everything you read is not going to be interesting, entertaining, or necessarily well-written**. When you find something especially boring or poorly written, challenge yourself to find the "take-away" in the piece – five or ten points that represent the essence of what the writer was trying to say in creating the written work. Think about how you might do it better.

- **Consider first why you are reading what you're reading**. What initially caught your interest? Is it holding your interest? If you are reading something you don't want to read or is on a subject that doesn't interest you, it is more likely you will be distracted and not absorb or retain much of what you read. Or, is the writing so good that you're reading it anyway?

- **Understand that your attention and concentration is required for good reading**. Don't expect to enjoy reading or get the most out of the material if you're tired, distracted, or trying to do other things.

- **Time matters**. If you don't allow yourself a reasonable amount of time to at least scan the material, expect you won't enjoy or remember it.

- **If you find yourself exploring a subject that's relatively new or really foreign to you...** Here's what works for me – begin by reading simplified, introductory material on the subject, not necessarily the most famous or definitive work which might be presented using more sophisticated or advanced terms. Work your way into it.

- **Don't feel obliged to finish every book you start**, unless, of course, there is some sort of requirement. But, again, try to understand why you didn't want to keep reading. That is always a lesson worth learning.

- **Scan or skim**. Sometimes it helps to work your way into a piece. You might even want to highlight or copy what appear to be significant points on a separate blank page that help you find the point of the writing. Remember that each paragraph is supposed to have a topic sentence. Consider its relative importance to the work.

- **Get a second opinion**. Consider the possibility that another written work can provide authoritative information on these points in a more interesting way.

General good advice for writers…

- Know your audience.
- Who are you writing for?
- What are you trying to say?
- What's your purpose for writing this?
- What can readers expect to get from reading your work – what's the take-away?
- Can you support your facts and have you clearly identified your opinions?
- Is your material organized or presented in such a way that the reader will get the point of the work without having to search for it?
- Can your writing be concisely summarized?
- Is the writing that surrounds or frames the concise summary useful, interesting or entertaining, or is it simply page padding?
- Finally, is your finished product something you would want to read yourself?

Good writing makes good reading. It not only contributes to the wealth of human knowledge, but provides a satisfying and rich experience to be savored by the individual reader.

It's none of their business that you have to learn to write.
Let them think you were born that way.
— **Ernest Hemingway**

My task... is, by the power of the written word
to make you hear, to make you feel – it is, before all, to make
you see. That – and no more – and it is everything.
— **Joseph Conrad**

It is better to write a bad first draft
than to write no first draft at all.
— **Will Shetterly**

By writing much, one learns to write well.
— **Robert Southey**

Part One:

It's about the Words

About Writing...

"Write what you know," the instructor said earnestly. Who could argue with that? The advice about writing seemed to make a lot of sense, even if it was a cliché as old as the word cliché. Despite having heard the phrase often, it made me remember my first job as an editor, when one of the things I had to do was evaluate manuscripts submitted for publication. I had my first experience with how valuable that advice could be.

The manuscript was for a detective novel, set in the era of the great old "hard boiled" pulp fiction stories of Dashiell Hammett, Mickey Spillane, and *Detective* magazine, all now long gone from the literary universe. The novel was written by a woman in her seventies. Two pages into it, three facts became clear: (1) she had never been a 37 year-old male private detective solving a "jewel heist" on "the grimy side of lower Manhattan" in 1935; (2) she really loved these kinds of stories; and (3) the novel wasn't very good.

As I wrote the rejection letter, I thought how much more interesting her manuscript might have been if she'd reframed the story with more of who she was and what she knew – perhaps a grandmother who had fantasies of being a mystery writer finding herself solving crimes. Years later, that would be the premise of a hit TV series titled *Murder, She Wrote*. Ah well… chalk it up as another great idea ahead of its time.

The point is, this woman was trying to write something she couldn't. She broke the "write what you know" rule. That's not to suggest that she could – or should – only write about being an old woman. After all, there are lots of things she must know. For example, she might use the classic *Readers Digest* setup and write about the most unforgettable character she'd ever met or

3

her worst summer or her first kiss, her greatest love, childhood Christmas, most embarrassing event, or worst fear. These were all things she knew and she could draw upon decades of memories of people and experiences, colorful, sad, funny, menacing, or unusual. It would not be necessary for her to become Sam Spade or Mike Hammer.

Or, if she actually knew someone who had been a detective or police officer way back then, she could write what that person knew. But, clearly, she hadn't. The simple fact remains, somehow, you have to know *something* of the subject you're writing about.

Library shelves are filled with excellent books about warfare by people who never fought in a war; books about Elvis by people who never knew him; and books about space travel by folks who have never been farther than Space Mountain at Disney World.

Historical volumes on Lincoln or Queen Elizabeth have been so richly done as to read like novels. There are tales of Camelot and stories about life on submarines or downhill racing so technically explicit as to convince readers the authors must be the world's most informed experts on their subjects. These are works by people who did research on their subjects so completely that, by the time they began writing, they were writing what they knew.

Many editors and publishers still insist that nonfiction writers have no business submitting novels or plays. By the same token, many feel that fiction writers are storytellers, not scholars, and should stay in their own fields – that they should all just write what they know.

Well, not exactly.

Robert Graves, Kurt Vonnegut, Joan Didion, Tom Wolfe, John Updike, and Erica Jong, to name six, proved that idea was empty generations ago. To use a baseball term, "they hit to all fields."

Kingsley Amis summed up the matter nicely with his comment that "any proper writer ought to be able to write anything from an Easter Day sermon to a sheep-dip handout."

We'll take his word for it regarding the sheep-dip handout.

For now, let's write about what I know. Though it might mean that, first, we'll have to learn about it.

A Writing Exercise

1. Now… write what you know

Write five things you know. They can include the name of a person who makes you smile or a person you find annoying; the worst job you ever had; a first impression of school; a place you've dreamed of visiting; one thing you would like to accomplish before you turn an age you consider old; or something else.

2. Next, pick one topic from the list.

Write 300 words on your subject of choice. Write it in first-person voice – make it be your true story. If it's a subject where you feel you need to know more, you will have to do a bit of research so you can write about it with accuracy and authority.

3. Conclude your piece with a statement that makes it meaningful.

Tell us why this subject is so significant to you and why we should care enough to read your account.

4. Bonus: List five topics about which you'd like to know more.

These are topics with which you'd like to become more knowledgeable. Perhaps you know a little already – like a favorite sport or musical group. Or maybe you'd just like to know more about some period of history… whatever. Then, over time, see if you can become more knowledgeable. You might want to start a file folder for each topic.

Writing for Public Communication...

...is a term encompassing all communications that might be read by others. These days, virtually all writing comes under this designation, with few exceptions. Even journals, diaries, or personal or business letters, that might seem as if they wouldn't qualify as "public," can be. Some are indeed of such a private nature that they should not be termed "public communications." Yet, they still involve the practice of writing and they do, in fact, often come to be read by others. Sometimes in this week's *National Enquirer.*

Consider this:

- Anne Frank's diary was published under the title *The Diary of a Young Girl* in 1947, two years after her death was confirmed by the International Red Cross. Her thoughts and experiences became a record of history that continues to touch readers more than a half-century later.

- A US senator's personal diary, in which he arrogantly, vainly, or stupidly – depending on one's point of view – chronicled his own misdeeds, was subpoenaed by the government and became the centerpiece in evidence that brought about his downfall.

- Hugh Prather's 1983 best seller, *Notes to Myself*, was not really intended to be read by only him. This collection of poems and random musings were notes that he intended on sharing with his publisher and anyone with three dollars or so at the time. He went on to similarly write *Spiritual Notes to Myself*, *Notes on Love and Courage*, *Notes to Each Other*, and several other volumes with titles suggesting they were not "public communications."

- A research study that involves technical and analytical applications might be intended as a component of a particular internal examination or project, yet it could become a published example of irrefutable findings of fact.
- E-mails are now routinely collected as evidence in court cases and are used to recreate timelines of events by researchers.
- Even jottings on the backs of envelopes can end up as public communication – Lincoln's Gettysburg Address is a notable example.

The Importance of Note-Taking

Does that mean notes to one's self need to be written in complete sentences, carefully punctuated, and mindful of the correct use of adjectives, gerunds, and editors' idiosyncratic peeves? Hardly.

It does, however, make a case for taking all of your writing seriously – even your note-taking. Understand that sometimes the most seemingly minor idea, thought, or observation could become not only significant, but perhaps career-changing or life-altering. If that seems an overstatement, it's not. Big ideas – important thoughts – come at unexpected times, and having a basic skill to frame such thoughts and put them down in writing is no trivial matter.

Major Areas of Public Communications

Typically, when people think of writing for public communication, newspapers, magazines, books, television and radio scripts, come to mind. Perhaps newer media forms such as Web sites, Internet copy, blog posts, and YouTube videos as well.

But consider other forms of writing that reach the public:

- Plays
- Film scripts
- Surveys, studies, white papers, and business communications

- Newsletters
- Songs
- Stand-up comedy acts
- Point-of-sale presentations – live or recorded
- Speeches
- Sermons
- Public service announcements
- Political campaign literature
- Catalog copy
- Instruction manuals
- Scripted tour presentations
- Scripted sales presentations
- Training programs
- Sales brochures and other literature
- Corporate annual reports
- Prerecorded phone or public address system announcements
- Greeting cards
- Trading cards
- Graphic novels (comic books)
- Theater and event programs/souvenir books
- Guide books
- Criticism [film, theater, TV, concert, book, record, or CD reviews]
- Commentary
- Packaging copy [text on boxes, bags, cans, bottles]
- Direct mail
- And there's more – you might want to add to the list yourself: _____

From the publication of your innermost thoughts, accidentally shared with the world when you hit the wrong e-mail key, to the back of breakfast cereal boxes and the liner notes for CDs and DVDs, writing for public communication is an ever-broadening platform for educating, informing, entertaining, and expression. If you write at all, some of that public communication will be done by you.

A Writing Exercise

Write a page in a journal or notebook or use a normal piece of paper or an electronic notebook page following this prompt.

1. The subject of your entry is "the public" as you choose to define it under Writing for Public Communication.

2. Who makes up your "public" – your family, a circle of friends, classmates, people you work with, a much larger constituent group?

3. Write a paragraph offering your opinion on "the public's right to know," as if the paragraph were being written to be read only by people you know personally.

4. Then write a paragraph on the same theme with the possibility in mind that someday your journal might be published and read by people you've never met.

5. Compare the two paragraphs and see if your tone, comfort level, and/or content changes between the two paragraphs. Is one of them, in your opinion, more persuasive or effective in making a strong argument for or against the public's right to information?

*My aim is to put down what I see and what I feel
in the best and simplest way I can tell it.*
— **Ernest Hemingway**

*A writer needs three things, experience, observation, and imagi-
nation, any two of which, at times any one of which,
can supply the lack of the others.*
— **William Faulkner**

*By speech first, but far more by writing, man has been able to
put something of himself beyond death. In tradition and in books
an integral part of the individual persists, for it can influence
the minds and actions of other people in different places and
at different times: a row of black marks on a page can move a
man to tears, though the bones of him that wrote it are long ago
crumbled to dust.*
— **Julian Huxley**

Writing Is a Form of Communication...

...as we have been told over and over again.

Not all that profound, is it? But, all too often, as we get into the process of writing, we disregard that simple truth. We think that, somehow, it doesn't apply to our particular piece of writing – whatever it is. This would be a good habit to lose, though it's easier said than done. Sometimes it can sneak up on you. Sometimes you feel that what you're communicating is so obvious and you want to make it so special, that somewhere along the line, the notion of communicating gets lost.

That is so wrong.

Every type of writing is some kind of communication – from a novel or a business plan to directions across town or a list of things to do today; from a stock certificate to an apartment lease; from a summons to appear in court to a valentine. In every example, a writer is communicating something to a reader: here's the story; here's the deal; I hate you; I love you; remember to buy peanut butter. From the big book written for history to the Post-it notes to ourselves, it's all about communicating.

You have to hold on to that single thought. When you write an ad, don't put aside the idea of communicating and think "sales pitch."

When you begin to write a speech, for yourself or someone else, don't get so wrapped up in the oration technique or what you'll wear that you lose that first and foremost thought – communicate. Whether you end up with the Sermon on the Mount, the "I Have a Dream" speech, or the recorded announcement on the use of an elevator in case of fire.

It's all about the writer or speaker communicating something to the reader or listener. All the forms of writing covered here are just different examples of something being communicated.

As such, whatever form it takes, your writing should be about something. It should have a point. Sure, put in all the extras – the warm welcome, the promise of value, the heartfelt pledge of all the things the writer or speaker will do... But first and foremost – remember what you are communicating.

In my view, it's okay to write an ad influenced by great advertising that has come before or to write a speech that recalls great speeches of the past. All that is perfectly fine for style and tone, but today, right now, in everything you write, the thing to remember is that you have to communicate something.

While you're at it, you might also want to remember that you may want to begin by getting the attention of your reader or listener. If you want to be read and remembered, it should be something someone cares about, wants to read, or to know. Communicate.

It needs to be about something.

It needs to have a point.

It needs to be interesting to the reader.

Detail makes the difference between boring and terrific writing. It's the difference between a pencil sketch and a lush oil painting. As a writer, words are your paint. Use all the colors.
— **Rhys Alexander**

If you're going to write, don't pretend to write down. It's going to be the best you can do, and it's the fact that it's the best you can do that kills you.
— **Dorothy Parker**

It is like a pudding. It has no theme.
— **Winston Churchill**

A Writing Exercise

1. Think of something you've heard in a speech, interview, or commentary – something that left an impression on you. What made it memorable?

2. Write your remembrance of that experience, and the things that help you remember it now.

Writing Is...

...one of the most intimate and lasting forms of personal contact. When a romantic moment ends, people usually pull away. A conversation can be held in memory until it's forgotten or, worse, remembered incorrectly. But not writing. Because we can revisit it and share it exactly. It has the power to stay in that most personal of places – the human mind.

As the writer, you get to say what you want to say. You get to reread it and change it. You can pump it up or tone it down. Add flowers or cut it to the bone. When you finally send it out into the world, it is your expression, your sentiments uninterrupted, communicated by you for posterity, for the record. And it enters that most personal of places – someone else's mind.

Then there's the other side of the relationship. As a reader, you hold the piece of writing in your hands, whether it is a book, a letter, a journal, or a joke. You make contact with it. You can read slowly and carefully or skim it as quickly as you can. Whether you tear it up, fold it, place it in a box, in a drawer, an envelope, on a shelf, in the trash, or send it along to a friend who might be interested, a contact has been made. And it has entered your mind.

We touch it. It touches us. The words we write, even if only intended to be read by a special friend, enter the world and finds a place in someone else's mind.

A Journey through My Library

I look over at my bookshelves, packed with volumes of different sizes and shapes, many signed by their authors. I'll take one off the shelf. It may be a book I've not yet read, one I've read and enjoyed, or something I can't remember reading.

Standing at my bookshelf, I recall someone saying that having a book in her home made her feel as if she had the book's author there as a guest, sitting off in a corner, resting against the shelf – Dickens, Fitzgerald, Hemingway, Dorothy Parker, Ann Rice, Amy Tan, Stephen King. What a wonderful guest list.

And the letters I've saved. As the years go by, even a "Wish you were here" post card turns into a treasure. Time seems to add to its value.

I've met Kurt Vonnegut and Martin Amis and David Lodge and Richard Russo and Carolyn, the housewife who wrote what some people considered pornographic paperbacks at her kitchen table… and Nick Basbanes, the columnist for *Biblio* magazine. He loved books so much that his first book was about people who love books.

Each book is a journey of the mind. Our libraries are a record of that journey. Learning, searching, moving about with people we've created, or defined, going to places we've discovered, is a most amazing way to live or travel.

Occasionally, I get mail from people who read something I wrote and want to tell me that – and perhaps a couple of other things. They feel like they know me, and, in a way they do. Because I wrote something that connected with them.

We can say what we want about writing to satisfy only ourselves or not caring what others think, but when someone reaches out to say how much he or she enjoyed what we did, or was touched by something we wrote, the experience is humbling and, at least for writers I've known, very, very satisfying.

A Writing Exercise about Reading

1. Tell us about something you read recently that made a connection. Maybe it made you laugh or made you angry? Did you tell others about it or just smile or fume and keep it to yourself? Write a few paragraphs that briefly summarize the subject of what was read and explain why you reacted to it as you did. Tell us about your response as a reader. Try to do it in less than 250 words.

2. Introduce us to your library. Yours may only be beginning (I've been working on mine for decades), but you'll already be able to give us a feel for the journeys you've taken and the connections you've made.

One of the really bad things you can do to your writing is to dress up the vocabulary, looking for long words because you're maybe a little bit ashamed of your short ones.
— **Stephen King**

Little words move men.
— **Winston Churchill**

Writing a News Story...

...was once considered the most noble of writing assignments. Journalism was a higher calling for writers. Reporting the news and protecting the public's right to know made us part of "The Fourth Estate." Once, it was commonly accepted that a writer or "J-School" graduate pursuing a career in the newspaper business was someone who took writing more seriously. News reporters were members of an elite. They were even identified as important by no less a written document than the Constitution of the United States.

Some of the most quotable remarks of Thomas Jefferson and Ben-Franklin are on behalf of a strong, free press.

Jefferson wrote, "Our liberty depends on the freedom of the press, and that cannot be limited without being lost," and, "Our citizens may be deceived for awhile, and have been deceived; but as long as the presses can be protected, we may trust to them for light."

As for Benjamin Franklin, he made a fortune as a printer. Clearly he knew the value of the written word.

A vigilant press keeps the people informed and keeps politicians honest. Strong stuff. At least, that's the concept.

Putting aside for a time the impact and responsibility of newspaper reporters, consider the role of the newspaper in civilized society – from presenting a daily update of the most significant events in the city, the nation, and the world to providing information on sports, the arts, births, deaths, politics, business, and the weather. There's even a platform for cultural excursions and diversions by way of comics, crosswords, photos of Hollywood starlets and star clusters just discovered by the Hubble telescope, the jumble, and the sudoku thing. The newspaper delivers all this to us every day.

None of this happens without journalists. (Well, maybe the sudoku.) Quality counts. The better their writing, the better the newspaper, and the better informed the public.

It's tempting to fixate on winning international awards, gaining lucrative book contracts, and achieving celebrity in the manner of Bob Woodward and Carl Bernstein, the now famous *Washington Post* "Watergate" reporters. Yet, most reporters are simply glad to do their jobs well – every day. Because good reporting and good writing remains the cornerstone of knowledge, if not of democracy itself... but there's more to the story.

Contrary to public perceptions, most newspaper stories do not find their way into print because reporters are ever vigilant, curious, and tuned-in to all that's going on. Certainly there are reporters on the international beat, but there is another whole tier working to bring us the news. They arrange briefings and press conferences, schedule interviews, and prepare press releases. It's public relations and very often it is the real story behind the news.

Public relations people bring information to reporters, detailing the latest occurrences in business, entertainment, sports, politics, government, science, and more. They may be attempting to create, raise, lower, or reinvent the profile of a person or entity. Interviews are offered, pushed, and arranged; background information is provided; subjects are positioned. Seeds are planted. Leads are offered.

But there's still a journalistic job to do. The integrity, professionalism, and skill of the writer determine whether the resulting story is fluffy publicity or real information, representing something of value for the reader.

The Newspaper Business Is Evolving.

In 1900, there were 2,326 newspapers in the United States. That number dropped to 1,748 in 1970; to 1,480 in 2000; and to 1,452 in 2005. Part of that drop is related to the economics of publishing a newspaper; another part of it is the proliferation of other news sources, such as cable TV and the Internet.

Some believe that a large reason for the drop in newspaper readership is that newspaper writers, editors, and publishers – separately and together – took their eye off the ball or, in this case, the reader. Maybe so. Maybe not. Others simply note that changing demographics, changing media habits, and even longer commuting times all play a part. They're right, but, for whatever reasons, it is a big change in the American media landscape. In fact, the change in the newspaper business is one of today's big stories.

A few more things to think about: First, the guidelines for good reporting are still pretty much the same as in the days of Franklin and Jefferson. Quality and clarity still count. And there's more quantity. Today, there are more media channels to write for (including blogs), even though the number of newspapers is shrinking.

Thinking about reporting the news?

Here are some useful guidelines:

- Look.
- Listen.
- Question.
- Challenge.
- Write what you see.
- Write about who did what, when, where, and why.
- Tell the story as you saw it or as you heard it or as it was described to you by more than one informed source.

- Read back what you have written, as if someone else had written it, and ask yourself if it's interesting – even compelling.
- Check the facts.
- Does the story make you want to know more about the person, people, or event?
- Will the reader be able to create a mental picture from what you have written?
- Will someone somehow be better for receiving the information?

When good content is presented well, everyone benefits – whether the writer has a serious dedication to serving the people's right to know, or simply a craftsman's commitment to supplying information in concise and dependable format. When we know more, it's a better world.

Thomas Jefferson would be proud. And so would "the First American," Benjamin Franklin.

A Writing Exercise

1. Choose a story from today's news – from a newspaper, broadcast or cable news, or the Internet. It can be "hard news" or a feature piece.

2. Identify the basic facts of the story – who, what, when, where, and why the story was worth knowing.

3. Imagine a very specific audience – upscale business professionals, college students, senior citizens, members of a specific profession or supporters of a cause. Try to make it an audience dramatically different, or much narrower, than the story's original audience.

4. Now rewrite the story in your own way. Try to do it in 250 words. Use the basic facts of the original story, but make it of particular interest to the specific audience you chose.

Writing What We Read

We made the point earlier that one characteristic good writers seem to have in common is that they love to read. And it shows. The more we read, the better we become at distinguishing good writing from bad writing – at least in structure and form, if not always in content.

As writers, we are influenced by what we read and by the style of writers we enjoy reading. So it's not surprising that most writers are initially influenced by their favorite writers. Then, gradually, more individualism of style emerges, and, as we write more, we get better at it. So it's not uncommon for writers to change their styles dramatically as they develop – or to develop a number of styles, depending on the assignment.

The journey may vary; but the destinations are often quite similar. The ultimate result is not only developing a writing style or a writer's voice, but being able to more effectively communicate.

Writing. Reading. They go together hand in glove. So it's not surprising that when we judge writing, we judge it by its readability. Here's a simple way to judge readability.

- Was it interesting?
- Did you want to read on?
- Were you able to take something away from it – to learn something from it?
- Simply put, did you feel it was worth your time?

It was Walt Disney who reportedly said that everything coming out of his company – movies, TV, books, music, and theme parks – had to both educate and entertain. Setting aside whether or not the Teacup ride achieves this objective, the rule is a good one –

especially for writers. Even though what actually constitutes good reading (and good writing) is, in fact, highly subjective. We know what we like. Generations expound on the brilliance of Dickens; others find him tedious. The same can be said of Chaucer and even (blasphemously) of Shakespeare. It happens. No matter that someone is declared the greatest writer in the history of the English language – ever – if a reader does not connect with a particular piece of writing, no amount of insistence will convince him or her it's great.

Some writing does not translate well through the generations. When language usage is dated or antiquated, it is difficult to get many in the next generation to read it, much less to accept its greatness. Sometimes, it takes more than one reading to "get it."

In the case of Shakespeare (once again, a good example), seeing the production of the play might be more powerful than reading the text. After all, some sniff, much of Shakespeare's work was written to be spoken by actors on a stage, not read silently in a classroom or library. A valid point. But let's remember the larger point – writing, be it the latest news story, or a joke as old as the hills, is storytelling.

So, what's your story? Whether the writing is fiction, nonfiction, graphic novels, poetry, or a magazine – including the ads – writing influences come from what we read and take in. Some may be inspired by Jane Austen, others by the *Onion*. What emerges from that inspiration, even if derivative, is invariably unique – at least to some degree. After all, the purpose is to communicate and we're using a language developed over the centuries. And some of our stories have been around for quite some time.

That said, as we tell our stories, we all tend to develop our "voice." The more writers write, the more unique and distinctive those voices become. And, if someday, someone should compare your writing to that of Fitzgerald, Hemingway, or even Stephen King, well, there are words of criticism that are worse to hear or read.

A Writing Exercise

1. Consider a piece of writing that was particularly memorable to you – something you really enjoyed. It can be a detective story, a sports story, an American Girl story, something from *The Babysitter's Club*, or a column from today's paper. It should be something quite a bit longer than 250 words.

2. Identify the essential elements of the piece you choose.

3. Write a 250-word synopsis of the piece. Try to emulate the style of the original writer.

4. Reread what you wrote and think about how much it resembles the work of the original writer and how much of yourself you think comes through in the writing.

I am a part of all I have read.

— John Kieran

Writing an Outline...

...is, unless the assignment or protocol requires it, a personal choice. While not ranking among the weightiest of life's personal choices, it is nonetheless a reflection of individual style and work habits. It is also a reflection of the project itself. An outline for a poem? Probably not. For a technical textbook? Maybe so.

When a writer asks if he or she should outline first, remember that some very successful writers insist they absolutely never outline their material, believing that to do so stifles their creative flow. Others, who are highly organized and know exactly where they want to go, what they want to do, and in what order, insist they could not work without first outlining their material.

Non-fiction, in most instances, seems to absolutely require an outline before the work can move forward. A good presentation of material must be organized. It is difficult to envision a proper history, a book on finance, a PowerPoint presentation, or any type of "how-to" effort being started, much less completed, without the structure preparing an outline imposes. However, when writing fiction, poetry, and humor, following where the muses and inner voices lead, an outline might seem to get in the way of the rhythm of the work or the creative flow.

Writers sometimes outline, but call it something else. The novel or short story has its plot; the stage play its presentation in three acts; the screenplay, with a formula incorporating key structural elements of both the novel and the play, has some surprising structural components. Ever hear of "beats?" Screenplays have them.

Even short writing has a bit of an outline structure. For example, a comedian's joke has its establishing premise, its set-up, and its punch line.

Beginning/middle/end. Exposition/conflict/resolution. Sound familiar?

Whether or not, you're writing an outline first, writers need to consider what it is they want to say, how they want to say it, and to whom they are speaking. This last point has a lot to do with the tone and degree of detail – creative or otherwise – that will go into the effort. For example, a biography of Abraham Lincoln could stretch over several volumes and offer minute details that present the total picture of the man, his life and times, and his principles. On the other hand, Jim Bishop's *The Day Lincoln Was Shot* focused on a brief period in an eventful life.

To state the obvious, some audiences require more, some less. In certain instances, volumes of research must be presented or summarized to validate a premise and sustain the credibility of the work. In other cases, little or no validation is required.

Knowing the audience, its expectations and demands, will determine much of what details are necessary – or unnecessary. That factor will influence the amount of research and organization that requires an outline and that an outline requires.

In fiction, your outline is essentially the plot. If a writer knows the plot of the story that will unfold, the writer has, in a basic sense, outlined the story, however unwritten or loosely formed that outline may be. Many fiction writers observe that once they begin writing, the characters' voices take over. In many cases, they – the writers – have no idea where the story is going or how it will end. Sometimes it works. Sometimes it doesn't. This technique can result in a bright, energetic, highly imaginative work or a rambling, disjointed, meandering product that some readers and critics may dismiss as unreadable. Then again, others may call it brilliant. For every reader who found James Joyce's *Ulysses* to be a work of rare genius, another said, "Huh?" and claimed not to understand it at all. Such is the course of fiction and the art of writing.

Know what you want to say. Know to whom you want to say it. Then, decide if having an outline will help.

A Writing Exercise

1. Choose a subject – a person, a place, an event, or a cause.

2. Write a free-form paragraph on that subject. Present as much detail as you can offer, following the journalism guideline of telling who, what, where, when, and why the subject is interesting or important to you.

3. Use that paragraph as a guide to create an outline for how you might present a larger article, essay, novel, or screenplay in an organized and logical way with information on the background, present, characteristics, and content with interesting or unique differentiating detail. You may want to lapse into prose as you describe your rationale and your project's possible future direction.

Finding Your Writer's Voice...

...can be an interesting and fascinating experience. As children, we mimic what we see – family members, characters on television – and as we get older we experience that unique brand of individualism that moves us to buy clothes, cars, even homes that seem to reflect both our individualism and the influences others have had on us.

The young rock band in the garage may start out emulating a favorite group. Getting up to deliver a speech or a report, a speaker may consciously or unconsciously mimic gestures and moves of other speakers he or she has seen and heard. Influences, noticed or unnoticed, are there.

Obviously, there is comfort in being a part of a group, while still retaining one's individual personality. That is certainly true of writers.

In the beginning, most writers don't mind being compared to other writers and, as in sports or music, there is invariably an unspoken rivalry, even among close friends. But after a while, those feelings change. Despite the fact that each writer has created something original, the competition for recognition is real. One more thing. As is also true of many other professions, writers' best friends are often other writers. The unspoken competition can be fearsome.

Much is written about how writing is a solitary, sometimes lonely business.. Rarely does collaboration produce writing of the quality each writer can produce alone. Though the ease of swapping text files may change that. And like other professions, there are associations, guilds, leagues, writers' conferences, retreats, and workshops – all opportunities to come together with so much in common, while fighting to be unalike, they make up an odd tribe, a band of brother and sisters going in different directions at varying speeds, watching each other to see who might have found a better way... and following after, hoping to arrive at a different destination.

As you write, you'll find that a transformation occurs – your writing voice emerges. Perhaps it comes from a personal experience or observation; maybe an epiphany or an entry in a journal that goes on longer than most other entries. The more a writer writes, the more personal his or her style becomes. Each writer develops a voice like no other. It's true of advertising copywriters, novelists, screenwriters, and poets.

But that transformation doesn't occur with a flash of magic, it comes from the continued use of words being set down in different ways, in different order, over different times. It makes writing a lot easier in many ways, but deepens the sense of self-criticism and alters the standards of judging quality. It's what makes certain writers so particularly good on certain subjects and explains why poets don't turn up writing great stage plays and why good journalists will usually write lousy ads.

Like practicing the piano or violin, repeated writing, rewriting, polishing, sharpening, and editing are needed... until a point is reached where it is clear that what is being written is so much better than what came before. Of course part of it is the truth in the old practice-makes-perfect adage, but when writers find their own voices is when other people ask them to take a look at some things they've written and perhaps offer a suggestion on how to make it better. It's a coming of age, again, and the satisfaction and confidence it brings can't be described; it must be experienced. And the experience is worth writing about.

A Writing Exercise

1. Find a major news story that has appeared in five places: a major daily city newspaper, a weekly news magazine, *USA Today*, the *Wall Street Journal*, the *Christian Science Monitor*, and, perhaps, the *Economist*, which has a slightly British point of view.

2. Read all five versions of the story.

3. Write a brief critique on the differences and distinctions you note in both the tone and content of the five stories. How many different voices were there?

4. Write a brief (100-word) synopsis of the story.

5. Try to determine which, if any, of the five articles most influenced your own version of the story.

My task... is, by the power of the written word to make you hear, to make you feel – it is, before all, to make you see. That – and no more – and it is everything.
— **Joseph Conrad**

Writing to Influence People...

...White Papers, Position Papers, and Policy Papers.
Let's start at the beginning. Whether you're trying to persuade a few influential decision-makers or the great mass commonly designated as "the general public," the title or headline of your piece is critical. It will determine whether or not the reader will start to read it – or move on. Writers try to influence their readers with their very first words. This is particularly true when you're trying to make your case.

You may not have read a position paper lately, but they can be hugely influential. For example, one of the main contributors to the establishment of the United States of America was a particularly effective piece of persuasive writing by Thomas Paine. It was called *Common Sense*, and it played a major role in shaping the thinking of our soon-to-be nation. It's quite a bit of writing – you might want to take a look. Even today, you can feel its persuasive power.

Alexander Hamilton and James Madison were two others that had great influence in helping to get our brand new country on the right track with their writings.

At an earlier time, white papers, position papers, and policy papers were serious, carefully prepared documents that served as definitive, often authoritative references on quality, value and economic justification. The authors of these documents were typically staff experts at government agencies, "think tanks," or research organizations. Today, that may no longer be the case.

Sometimes, that expert is you – and you may not feel like much of an expert. Here are some thoughts to get you started.

White Papers

For a long time the announcement that someone had issued a "white paper" suggested that something very important and official had been released. The term white paper had that ring to it – like an edict or a proclamation. However, as the saying goes, times change.

Many professionals in the field of public relations today believe that what is called a white paper is basically a corporate brochure in another format. It might not be a proclamation, but the term white paper still sounds a whole lot more impressive than "brochure."

And, when running a PR campaign, it may be that you need to get some important and complex thoughts in front of "thought leaders." If so, you might need a white paper.

A white paper on a specific subject is, in fact, a standard tool in marketing communications. Many decision-makers use them as primary sources of information, believing white papers are an effective way to educate, inform, and, most importantly, to influence prospective customers – with (still) a reasonably high credibility as source material. Even though we recognize that the designation may be largely superficial, it is, at its best, a pure intellectual argument that operates at as high a level of thinking as possible – given the audience. A white paper should reinforce why the thoughts and philosophy of the person or organization that produces it should be chosen over some competitive point of view. Remember, there is still a marketplace of ideas – your white paper could play an important role.

A company or organization today might use a white paper to:

- introduce or position something as innovative
- demonstrate knowledge of today's challenges
- emphasize the uniqueness and advantages of its solution
- influence decisions

- form the foundation of or contribute to a marketing strategy,
- demonstrate the force of a solution, rather than simply hype a product.

According to Michael A. Stelzner, "White papers are at the forefront of an educational marketing revolution." Mr. Stelzner should know, having written a book on the subject, an ongoing blog, and white papers for Microsoft, FedEx, Motorola, Monster.com, Hewlett-Packard, and SAP, among others. He compares white papers to other types of reports and notes that both reports and white papers tend to be longer forms of writing, and are often heavy on text and contain few graphics

White papers and reports have distinctions and differences, in that they:

- both include informative and persuasive information
- are usually written by a company or individual for promotional purposes
- are often used directly in a sales-related program, such as to generate leads or as a leave-behind piece
- take a very specific position
- discuss processes in detail
- often examine benefits of a solution, and
- might include examples or applications.

Reports simply present the facts, but white papers sell a particular point of view. Stelzner also believes a report is much closer to an article, as it includes information and facts about topics and does not usually attempt to sell any one idea or concept. White papers, he notes, add the persuasive element by pointing readers down a very specific path.

Experts suggest that to develop a white paper, a writer should begin with a well-developed overview, executive summary, or abstract that captures the target audience's attention.

It should include a critical one-paragraph summary and provide information that gives the reader a reason to read further, keeping in mind that many people read by jumping to the end paragraphs or conclusion before reading the entire contents of a document. The challenge is for the writer to do what writers are supposed to do: make the material interesting.

Just as filmmakers might shoot many additional scenes to get a short sequence that works, writers of anything – articles, reports, profiles, brochures, or white papers – must read, research, study, and dig to end up with the nugget of data from which an interesting block of material can emerge.

The final product should, at the very least, inform, educate, and entertain. A great deal of mining might need to take place before getting a nugget of gold.

State the problem and…

- identify the main objectives of the paper;
- write two or three paragraphs showing your knowledge of current challenges and trends;
- don't make assumptions without validation;
- avoid having a hidden agenda – people know others want something; there's no value in pretending that's not the case;
- avoid technical, complex terms, acronyms, etc., and define those that can't be avoided.

Describe the subject and explain why, considering such things as design decisions, industry standards, testing, reliability, and best practices, the solution is the right one.

While the white paper of the 21st century is still represented as being authoritative, it is just as likely to be written by a corporate public relations practitioner, PR agency staff, or a freelance writer with access to company files. Just as an advertorial is a paid ad that will attempt to make a company or organization's case by adopting the format and tone of a newspaper editorial, employing a presumed industry or expert perspective and not mentioning the company or product by name, a white paper follows the tone and format of a government or academic study, while essentially offering the same content found in a company brochure, but without the company name or logo. Indeed, some critics have even described the modern white paper as a corporate brochure in all but the packaging.

Whether or not such presentations are ethical, questionable, or merely a reflection of modern marketing positioning techniques can be held for another forum. In terms of the writing, the white paper, position paper, or policy document represents another opportunity for a business or academic writer to present a point of view on a company, organization, or product that can be positioned, defended, and responsive to concerns or criticism. An effective communicator can address the challenge and present a body of information in either a scholarly, official, or conversational tone, as the subject demands.

Public relations is about presenting a message in a persuasive and effective way. The white paper provides an excellent vehicle to do exactly that.

Write what you want to read. The person you know best in this world is you. Listen to yourself. If you are excited by what you are writing, you have a much better chance of putting that excitement over to a reader.
— **Robin McKinley**

Whatever you can do, or dream you can, begin it;
Boldness has genius, power and magic in it.
— **Johann Wolfgang von Goethe**

A Writing Exercise

1. Choose a six-panel or more corporate brochure on any subject where a product, service, or cause is involved, such as banking, travel, petroleum, dentistry, pharmaceuticals, or a social or political movement.

2. Read the brochure.

3. Using the brochure as a basis document, write a white paper – an authoritative opinion essay that begins with a thesis statement and ends with a conclusion based on an examination of facts and opinions cited – of no more than four pages (typewritten, double-spaced, 1" margins all around, using a 12-point Times Roman font).

For example, if it is a cruise brochure, perhaps you might write something on the superiority of a cruise as a vacation decision, or how a cruise can revitalize a relationship. If it is a corporate brochure, how about an essay on the larger importance of their product category or economic activity.

4. Do not refer to any company, product, or organization by name; allow your presentation and conclusion to be subject-focused, rather than company-specific.

Writing with Style…

…sounds like something good – something classy. Style is one of those words, like beauty or grace, that is applied as a compliment, even though it is in fact a highly subjective term, defined very much in the eye of the beholder. And, for whatever reason, to be said to lack style has a very definite disapproving, dismissive connotation.

Most of us will be in that middle ground, alternating between compliments and criticism, until we receive that second Pulitzer Prize or have a fifth best-seller make the New York Times list. Until then, a writer will most likely be asked what other writers most influenced his or her style.

For some unique writers, their style lives on. Here's a favorite example. Every year since 1978, Harry's American Bar and Grill in Century City, California, has asked people to submit one page of writing in the style of Ernest Hemingway, with the winning entrant receiving round-trip airfare and dinner for two at Harry's American Bar and Grill in Florence, Italy, reportedly once a favorite spot of the late author. Now called the International Imitation Hemingway Contest, the competition was for years referred to as the "bad Hemingway" competition. Participants not only had to emulate the style of the legendary writer, but they had to make it fun, even daring to satirize Hemingway in the process.

Hemingway is an author who projected a personal sense of style as well as a literary style. And even people who have not read his words accept the designation of him as "stylish" without argument.

For his thirteenth book, another successful writer created a novel with a Christmas theme. He hoped it would stay around forever, he said. When a friend congratulated him on turning out a fine book, the writer replied, "It's sort of in the style of P.G. Wodehouse."

As it happened, this particular friend had read a lot of Wodehouse's work and found the only similarity between the two was that both writers were printed on white paper. So who missed on the style issue? The writer? The friend? Wodehouse? It didn't matter. The style and degree of influence was in the eye of the beholder. Perhaps they were all right.

Elsewhere, the head of an ad agency met a friend on the street and said his business was going great. He wanted to bring the work to a point where people could see it and say, "That's a (blank) agency ad."

The friend paused, then asked rather innocently, "Shouldn't the ad focus on the client's product or company and its particular style and image, rather than that of the ad agency?" The executive's complexion briefly changed color and the subject was quickly shifted, but the look in his eyes said he hoped his friend would be hit by both a bolt of lightning and a city bus, ideally at the same moment, before the sun went down.

In writing copy, particularly for advertising, emulating the style of another writer can be risky business, possibly falling somewhere between plagiarism and reaching an audience that doesn't share an appreciation for the style of the writer being copied.

The ad should present the facts – the who, what, when, where, why, and how of the subject and make a "value statement." That is, the reader should be presented with a clear reason to care about the product and take the next step of going out to look for it. No one ever accused the writers of leases or financial reports of being creative or of having a nice writing style. Perhaps the authors of these documents were highly creative people, who could put just the right tone or spin on ad copy and poetry, but knew creativity should be applied appropriately and should not be at the expense of critical information. Something more stylish might fit nicely in the writer's portfolio, but it will not be of much value to either the client or the reader looking for help in making key decisions.

As you work to develop your own writing style, here is some general good advice that can help you go in the right direction…

Writers' Tips for Other Writers on Writing

- Put your reader first when writing something intended to be read by others. You are the storyteller – even when you are also the story.

- Write for people, even if your reader is only one person. Communicate in a way that can be understood.

- Organize your thoughts, information, and important points in a logical manner.

- Write in short paragraphs and try to avoid long texts that turn-off readers. The most expressive writing falls far short if no one wants to read it.

- Write short sentences as they tend to be clearer and more focused.

- Use words and terms readers will understand without breaking the stride of reading to consult a dictionary.

- Be concise for greater clarity.

- Be specific, especially in nonfiction, speechwriting, and in ad copy.

- Make your point early and keep coming back to it.

- Writing in a conversational style makes readers feel involved.

- Avoid language that is offensive or sexist. Sometimes such an approach is done intentionally to make a point, but if the reader does not perceive what the writer is trying to do, the result can be negative. Either way, writing to shock or unnerve a reader is more genre writing and does not belong in mainstream communications.

- Enjoy the process of expressing yourself, even with others' words.
- Put yourself in the reader's place to judge the quality of what you write.

A Writing Exercise

1. Turn to the work of a single writer who has written both fiction and nonfiction (such as John Updike, Joan Didion, or Philip Roth). Read a page of each and note if the writer appears to have altered his or her style.

2. Next, read a page of writing on the same subject by another writer.

3. Note the differences in style between the same author writing fiction and nonfiction and two authors writing on the same subject.

Observe, don't imitate.
— **John M. Ford**

All the words I use in my stories can be found in the dictionary –
it's just a matter of arranging them into the right sentences.
— **Somerset Maugham**

If I lose the light of the sun, I will write by candlelight, moonlight,
no light. If I lose paper and ink, I will write in blood on forgotten walls.
I will write always. I will capture nights all over the world and
bring them to you.
— **Henry Rollins**

Writing Time...

...is an area of concern to writers as well as to many readers. People never seem to have "the time" to do the things they need and want to do. Aspiring writers seem fascinated to know how long something took to write, where other writers prefer to write, what time of day works best for writing...

If you think about it, some of the most often used figures of speech are about time, such as:

It's about time!

I don't have time!

I need more time.

Doing time.

Making time (there's more than one application of this phrase).

Writers ask other writers how much time they spend writing (the only answer to this is, deadlines notwithstanding, however long it takes) or how they manage their time.

Do they write better early in the morning or late in the evening? As if there were a magical time of day when words come easier.

Time waits for no one.

Time keeps on slipping, slipping... into the future...

J.D. Salinger is said to have written eight hours a day – a shift, a regular day's work, a job. Some writers believe their time to write is whenever or wherever the Muse speaks to them. Hmmm.

Well, I guess you can wait for the Muse to arrive – but I've found that deadlines usually show up way before the legendary

Muse of literary inspiration. And that's why, mostly, writers seem to write to their deadlines. Busy people always seem to find time – to make time – for whatever needs to be done. Some will insist they are morning people or that they are not morning people. Others believe strongly they are night people. Well, as young folks like to say… whatever.

If your body tells you it is time to wake up, sleep, eat, exercise or rest, you probably ought to listen – at least until that Muse shows up. it is certainly possible that body chemistry can help dictate when it's time to write. But, like the all-nighters pulled right before exams or the "second wind" a very tired person seems to get when receiving a call from someone whose company is enjoyed, a good writer has at least one more gear – override. It's probably a good idea to use that gear every once in a while, as well.

In general, set aside a regular time to write. Too much time thinking about writing (I really have to get to this project, etc) doesn't tend to help. Try to write as often as you can – even if you're not staring at a deadline (or it's breathing down your neck). You'll have a better time of it.

That said, the very best time to write is when you need to meet a deadline or a due date because that's when the writer *must* overcome lethargy or procrastination and simply get it done. When writers are inspired or motivated to put words on paper without a deadline or a reason to do it, there somehow always seems to be time.

For those who say they have been thinking about writing a book or a story someday and will do it when they have the time… well, that time will probably never come. Because the truth is, that need or desire to actually write is a lower priority in their lives. So the problem really isn't one of time, it's one of actually wanting to write.

You've got to want it.

And, if you want it, in the words of the popular Nike ad campaign, "just do it."

A Writing Exercise

1. For one day, keep a log of all you do – a minute-by-minute account of your day. If that seems too difficult, do it for a half-day.

2. At the end of the period, note how productive you were – or were not. Everyone is entitled to take breaks, enjoy idle conversation, and just experience some "down time."

The point of this exercise is to help you get a sense of how much time most people either waste or can't account for, or overspend on many of the things they do. In this situation, it's not about determining the correctness of the time spent or wasted; it's about understanding clearly that time is manageable and a lack of it shouldn't be a scapegoat for things not accomplished. Like writing.

> *If you don't have the time to read,*
> *you don't have the time or the tools to write.*
> — **Stephen King**

> *I hate writing; I love having written.*
> — **Dorothy Parker**

> *Beginning writers must appreciate the prerequisites if they hope*
> *to become writers. You pay your dues – which takes years.*
> — **Alex Haley**

Writing Something That Will Be Read by Others...

...as in a proclamation, speech, or particularly important piece of writing representing something larger than just the view of the writer, as in a white paper or a policy document. Here's the challenge. The writing process is personal – while you're writing, it's for an audience of one. You have to translate that experience into one that crosses the line and interacts with an audience. How do you want to interact with that audience?

Will you try to persuade your audience – to come around to a particular point of view, or will you be affirming something they already believe? (We all know which is easier.) What tools will you use? The rhythm of your words? The power of your logic? A play on the heart strings?

William Wordsworth wrote poetry that spoke to finding and holding deep philosophical thoughts that would guide the reader through days to come. Wordsworth wanted to influence his readers with beautifully arranged words that found their way into people's hearts. A novelist wants the reader to connect with a story's main characters – at least one of them – to be pulling for that character to come out all right. And the novelist "paints a picture with words" to help the reader feel a part of the story.

Are you using the right words? It's critical. The legendary publicist Benjamin Sonnenberg looked for the right words to communicate, to excite, to influence, and to persuade the reader or listener to choose one product, brand or name from a sea of seeming equals.

Since the "others" who read your writing might have a few tough questions to ask, you might want to start by asking yourself a few.

Do the facts all add up to indisputable truth?

Do the words you use strike an emotional chord? Discounting facts, do you give the reader "permission to believe" what you are proposing?

Does the writing ask the reader to suspend disbelief?

Writing can communicate on many levels. To be most persuasive, you first have to write words that make sense. How do you find that out? Ask others if they think your writing makes sense.

Ask, "What's the point?"

Find out if it's persuasive. It's a tough world out there – find out if you really accomplished your mission. Did it register at all at doing what you wanted it to do?

If the answer is "no" or "maybe not," perhaps something more is needed. Maybe some different words. Maybe, if you want to get someone to change their mind, you might even start by agreeing with them – acknowledge the other person's point of view, and they'll be more inclined to listen to yours.

And don't feel down if you didn't get it done the first time – really successful writers learn as they write – and they get better. Lots better.

The basic tool for the manipulation of reality is the manipulation of words. If you can control the meaning of words, you can control the people who must use the words.
— **Philip K. Dick**

A Writing Exercise

1. Write a short piece (no more than 100 words) in which you attempt to persuade the reader to agree with your position – whether it is about recycling, exercising extreme caution in certain types of situations, or supporting a candidate or cause.

2. Offer facts to support your argument.

3. Reread your finished argument and ask yourself if it *communicates*, *excites*, *influences*, and *persuades* the reader to accept your point of view.

If not, how can you rewrite it to strengthen your case? Is there a powerful story? Can you use logic or a persuasive example? Is there some data or other factual reference to help make the points you need to make for effective persuasion?

If you can't annoy somebody, there's little point in writing.
— **Kingsley Amis**

In brief, I spend half my time trying to learn the secrets of other writers – to apply them to the expression of my own thoughts.
— **Shirley Ann Grau**

Writing "New Journalism"...

These days, the term "new journalism" isn't used as much as during its first decade or so, but it is still around and an interesting alternate approach to the "old journalism." Previously, journalism was simply journalism – objectively recording and reporting events as they happened. In journalism as it was, the writer never used the person pronouns. The word "I" had no place in journalism, unless someone was being quoted. The journalist was the observer, the chronicler, the narrator or storyteller.

In the new journalism, the writer is part of the story – personalizing each observation with comments and opinions. In new journalism, the story includes the storyteller. And that adds a new dimension in narrative – and in writing – because the writer's style can be a part of the narrative as well. It's no longer J-School journalism. Writers start sentences with "and" or "but" because it just seems to work when conveying a particular type of message. But sentences that begin with conjunctions and end in prepositions are the least of the writer's problems.

Although the new journalism isn't so new anymore, it has become another way of approaching a story. It was created in the 1970s by writers, most of whom are now well into their seventies, if they are still alive at all.

Tom Wolfe, Norman Mailer, Gay Talese, George Plimpton, Hunter Thompson, and Truman Capote are a few of the most notable practitioners, if not the actual inventors. They are all fine writers, who for many years seemed to have turned out successful books and articles before they went "new." And, if the parade that followed in their footsteps isn't all of the same quality, still, it's an approach that some writers may find to their liking.

The term new journalism isn't used as much as it was during its first decade or so, but it is still around – primarily in feature writing and in books, where, in my opinion, not having enough materials for a book, the writer adds the narrative of all he or she went through to write the book to build the page count. Hey, maybe I should try it. Think of the spellbinding narrative I could add as I battle traffic in my Toyota to get to my writing class in time to deliver that eagerly awaited lecture… Hmmm. On second thought, maybe it's not for me. But it might work for you.

See what happens when you consciously make yourself part of the story – personalizing each observation with comments and opinions. That's the idea. In new journalism, the story includes the storyteller.

Blogs are a great example of this, often evolving into pure opinion offered as fact. Journalism should be better than that. And the good writers who started it all… Wolfe, Mailer, Capote, Talese, and Plimpton knew better.

It's different now. The story's not just about the story, it's about the writer's perspective or opinion – or the opinions of some other people who are not actually part of the story, but have something to say about it anyway. The justification is that this approach can add some interest or excitement to the story. Maybe so.

When the reader gets the first-person account of someone who was actually part of the story, it does exactly that – the same way we try to involve someone in the plot of a novel. The reporter becomes the protagonist that we identify with. Though some would argue that we're not talking about crafting engaging works of fiction but reporting the facts. For this, some journalists have quotation marks to frame the personal comments and opinions. For others, well we'll just put those quotation marks around "new journalism" and realize that the world changes and sometimes that means new opportunities.

The "journalism" part of journalism is still who, what, when, where, and why. And, to editorialize a bit myself, I feel that's the way it should be. Personal observations and opinions have a place – memoirs, editorials, and columns. Or at least that's how it used to be.

But times change. As you move ahead, you may discover that you are an old-school journalist, a new journalist, or maybe both.

A Writing Exercise

1. Recall a personal situation in which you were involved during the past 24 hours – anything from a class you attended or a day spent working, to your own reactions to something else that happened in the news, an incident witnessed or a report of something that impressed you, annoyed you, or was in any way thought-provoking.

2. Turn it into a news story in classic journalism style. Write an account of it in no more that 250 words in the third-person – as a news reporter might write it, noting who, what, when, where, and why. You can use quotes from people involved to add, color, drama, or perspective. Don't quote yourself in this version.

3. Now write a first-person, "new journalism" version of the same story. Add yourself to the story. Add some dramatic narrative that includes you. Add your own editorial voice.

4. Note the differences. Either approach is correct, but only the first version is journalism. What are some of the devices that you used – or didn't use – as you went between "old" and "new" journalism?

Writing Something
to Be Remembered…

… is not a motive many writers will admit to having. Of course, any worthwhile presentation of information should be remembered for its content or value by someone, hopefully, but the words or phrases that end up in the books of famous quotations are in a class by themselves.

Very few of these memorable and well-remembered lines are what lawyers call "spontaneous utterances." President Kennedy's classic call to Americans to "Ask not what your country can do for you; ask what you can do for your country…" is one of the most remembered and quoted lines from the previous century.

People who never even heard the entire speech regard Dr. Martin Luther King Jr.'s "I Have a Dream" as one of the truly outstanding contributions to both prose and social discourse in our time.

Did Dr. King know his words would echo through history, louder than so many millions of other words spoken or written? Was that particular speech recognized when it was created as "the one"?

Dr. King's words, like those of many religious leaders, operated on many levels – literary, spiritual, and inspirational – whether spoken or written. Writing words that would be spoken aloud, as well as pages that would be read silently, carries a challenge. The speaker knows the words heard and read will be analyzed and interpreted not only for their value and clarity of message, but for their ability to resonate with listeners and form bonds with readers days or years later.

When Dr. King said the words, "I have a dream," he hit a responsive note with audiences, young and old, scholars and dreamers alike, around the world. He would dare to dream and challenged others to do so. Most people, having dreams of their own, could relate to what he was saying, as well as to the power of his message

A well-considered, well-written presentation of information is useful. But when it reflects a *vision*, when it *reaches across barriers* so that what is said or written can bring writer, speaker, listener, and reader to a shared place, it becomes important and memorable – or as Shakespeare wrote, such stuff as dreams are made on.

Good writing is supposed to evoke sensation in the reader. Not the fact that it is raining, but the feeling of being rained upon.
— E.L. Doctorow

Some men see things as they are and ask why. Others dream things that never were and ask why not.
— George Bernard Shaw

Our lives with all their miracles and wonders are merely a discontinuous string of incidents – until we create the narrative that gives them meaning
— Arlene Goldbard

Everything changes when you change.
— Jim Rohn

A Writing Exercise

1. Think of a speech you have heard or read or a particular piece of writing – perhaps even only a quotation – that you found memorable or inspiring.

2. Write that quote or a quote from what you recall.

3. Write, in no more than 250 words, why you find what you have chosen memorable or important. Express yourself in the strongest possible terms.

4. Go back and Identify a passage or quote in what you have written that embodies or expresses your sense of the importance of what you observed.

Bonus: The Maria Rivera Post Card Project. For her birthday, writer and teacher Maria Rivera created an interesting project. She wrote, e-mailed, and even prepared a video tape requesting that a long list of her friends send her a post card for her birthday. On that post card, you would submit one piece of good lifetime advice. It could be a quote from others, a saying from your mother, or something you wrote yourself. Then, Maria collected all of these quotes and post cards and put them into an online album she shared. You might want to do the same at some time in your life. Collect and share the wisdom of your friends – and see what it takes to write something that is remembered.

Writing Letters...

...may seem like a process so routine that to spend very long thinking about it seems silly. That there are dozens of books published on How to Write a Letter seems even more absurd.

It's only a letter, for heaven's sake! We know the drill.

"Hi Mom, Having a great time at camp. Thanks for the cookies," or "Hey Dad, college is great; everyone here's been great; can you send the check by FedEx?" or "We'll be arriving with the whole gang Saturday morning and are really looking forward to spending a few months with you..."

In the world of writing, publishing, archiving, and generally creating inspired and powerful volumes to survive the ages, the letter has been pretty much dismissed – almost to the status of "afterthought." Certainly in this day and age, not a lot of planning, conceptualizing, editing, testing, or examination is devoted to letters, and much of what there is has been taken over by the ubiquitous e-mail. This is too bad.

If this book does nothing more than help you to get back in the habit of writing letters, I feel that, together, we will have helped make the world a better place. Your mother would certainly agree.

Looking at the field of letter-writing in general, consider it as falling into six general categories:

- **The Personal Letter** – one you write to friends and family;

- **The Letter to the Editor** – an opinion, a complaint, something worth sharing with "those in authority;"

- **The Annual Newsletter** – once a year, a way to stay in touch with all those who want to keep in touch with you;

- **Classic Correspondence** – maybe not on a level with Thomas Jefferson or John Adams, but sharing great thoughts with others is a useful human activity that, to date, has brought us some valuable insights, and is a tradition that should continue;
- **The Direct Mail Letter** – beginning with the appeal for more funds during your freshman year, this is actually a large and important industry;
- **The Cover Letter** – a surprisingly valuable tool even in this e-mail-driven 21st century.

Let's take them one by one.

The Personal Letter. This may be the toughest – at least at the beginning. A phone call is quicker. Our lives are not exactly competitive in drama with the evening news or the *National Enquirer* and what is it that we can say about ourselves? Well, here's an initial hint – tell the person you're writing to how you feel about them. Do you miss them? Do you remember (fondly, sadly, or with a bit of laughter) some moment you shared together? That lunch or dinner? Your last visit, which was too long ago, or the visit coming up – the one you're looking forward to. You'll find that once you involve the other person in your "personal" letter, you actually do have quite a bit to say. Then, add what bits and pieces of news and views you have laying around and you'll have something worth the price of a stamp.

I know an e-mail is cheaper and a phone call is faster, but it won't be saved and it won't have the same personal value. And, as writers we do want some of what we write to be remembered, don't we?

The Letter to the Editor. People writing angry letters have initiated periods of open-ended hostility, and it makes for interesting reading in our newspapers and magazines. During the "Cold War," governments got in the act, exchanging "strongly worded letters of protest" prolonging animosity. Bonds have been sealed

54

or severed through a short letter, beginning, ending or changing careers, lives and relationships. Nonetheless, sometimes we feel that the letter must be written. One reason they're usually interesting reading is that the writer has strong feelings on the topic. There's a lesson there for all of us – strong feelings make for powerful writing.

The Annual Newsletter. OK, once a year, is that too much to ask? If you want to e-mail it to everyone after you finish writing it, you have my permission. But think about what a nice tradition this is – to share your thoughts, a bit of wit, maybe a photo or two – perhaps with a caption ("That's all of us in front of Mount Rushmore. We never realized how much Aunt Rose looks like Teddy Roosevelt."), and whatever else happened during the calendar year. Get in the habit. It's a tradition that your friends and family will appreciate. Who knows, they might even send you a nicer gift next year.

Classic Correspondence. These days may be gone, but just as we see others perform historic recreations, perhaps some of you will help revive what is truly an art form. Letters that contain great thoughts, profound ruminations, and an ongoing dialogue that enriches us all years later. There are classic examples of these exchanges – the HBO series on John Adams noted the fascinating correspondence of John Adams and Thomas Jefferson. We can't all become pen pals with ex-presidents, but perhaps there is someone you'd like to engage in a dialogue of correspondence. Think about it? If someone comes to mind, write a letter.

The Direct Mail Letter. The Direct Mail industry is huge and, as important as the mailing list is, for a direct mail campaign to succeed everything really rests on the strength of the letter and the offer it communicates. The best list, the most willing prospect, the most receptive reader, can be turned-off or suddenly become quite disinterested in an offer or a proposal if it is presented by a written appeal to the reader. To date, the most effective vehicle for that appeal is still… the letter.

The Cover Letter. Any writer seeking an introduction to a publisher will readily attest to the importance of the cover letter. What about the millions of résumés sent every year? Mostly formatted to look the same, their only real distinguishing characteristic is their cover letter. Days and dollars may be invested in writing a terrific résumé, only to have it sent with a cover letter so devoid of interest or style as to doom the résumé to go unread, or, at best, filed in the unexceptional pile.

The cover letter is, potentially, some of the most important writing you will do in your career. Almost every proposal – for a service contract, a job, a legal settlement, anything – actually begins with its cover letter. Think it through; take it seriously.

Although the cover letter is generally written after the material it is supposed to introduce is completed, remember that this is the first contact the recipient will have with a proposal or submission, there's a lot depending on its being well received. First impressions are created; opinions are formed; trust or credibility can be enhanced or diminished.

A cover letter should be brief and straightforward – it should not be a verbatim repetition or excerpt from the information it is being used to introduce. If possible, it should be somewhat personal – in that it is clearly directed to the recipient, not some generic "to whom it may concern." If "To Whom" is the only name available, do what you can – but remember, your reader will be as removed from the message as you are when you get a letter with that kind of impersonal beginning.

Consider the cover letter an opportunity to briefly make points or list facts or strengths or to refer to names of others who might add weight to the content, but might be inappropriate or difficult to weave into an accompanying proposal or presentation document. The letter becomes doubly important if it arrives as a stand-alone communication, without a proposal or other document enclosed.

What is unique or special about the proposal or organization should be noted in the letter. It is a key selling vehicle that can also serve as a "teaser" to create heightened interest in the content that follows.

You may wish to close your letter on a friendly note, adding a light or personal touch. While a proposal is a communication outlining what one person or organization can do for another, the letter is a message from the writer to its recipient. Try to establish a friendly, yet businesslike positive connection between the proposal and person or people who will be reviewing it. By sending the proposal you are offering a commitment and asking for business. Try to convey, on a professional level, how important you regard that responsibility in a letter that reads as if its writer is someone whom the reader would like to meet for coffee, perhaps to hear more about what the writer has to offer.

If you can become a better letter writer, in one or all of these categories, you will be making the world a better place – all for the price of a stamp.

A Writing Exercise

In this section there are probably too many exercises to do in one sitting (but think of how much better a writer you'd become if you did do all of these exercises). Your instructor or writing coach may give you a less daunting list.

1. **The Personal Letter.** You've been meaning to write someone, haven't you? Well, now you have an excuse. Don't know how to start? Tell them it's a class exercise. Get going. Far more time is wasted thinking about writing a letter than has ever been spent actually writing it.

2. **The Letter to the Editor**. Quick, list your biggest pet peeve or the thing that irritates you the most. Try to hold onto that emotion. Now write a letter to the most appropriate person or group – the Complaint Department (these days we call it Customer Service), the Editorial Board, or your favorite (or least favorite) talk show host.

3. **The Annual Newsletter**. Why not start writing one? Start a file – collect a few snapshots, jot down some notes, and look for the newsletter formats on your computer (most word and page design programs have very nice templates). And don't forget to send us one.

4. **Classic Correspondence**. We'll merely ask you to think about it. So… write down the name – or names – of the most interesting thought-provoking people you know.

5. **The Direct Mail Letter**. Consider how a print ad has a headline to get the reader's attention and a TV or radio ad has only a few seconds to keep someone from leaving a room or changing a station.

- Apply this same principle of grabbing interest in seconds to a letter.
- Write a letter of no more than 100 words telling the reader why you should be the person chosen to create a communications plan for him or her or a company.
- Use "action" words, facts, comparisons, anecdotes, and a friendly, respectful, persuasive tone.
- Reread the letter asking yourself, if you were the person receiving it, would you act favorably upon it.
- If not, try to identify what interesting or persuasive points the letter lacks and rewrite it.

6. **The Cover Letter**. Have all the Direct Mail principles in mind from the previous part of these exercises when you write a cover letter for your résumé.

Writing for adults, you have to keep reminding them of what is going on. The poor things have given up using their brains when they read.
Children you only need to tell things to once.
— **Diana Wynne Jones**

Have something to say, and say it as clearly as you can.
That is the only secret.
— **Matthew Arnold**

Those who write clearly have readers.
Those who write obscurely have commentators.
— **Albert Camus**

To me the greatest pleasure of writing is not what it's about, but the music the words make.
— **Truman Capote**

Writing Criticism...

...is something a modest person might have a problem with, but actually it creates a lot of work for writers. Maybe we didn't write that screenplay, but in newspapers across the country, there is a need for movie reviewers who can translate the experience for readers wondering which movie to see on a Friday night. Even though, being judgmental about others' work seems, well, rude actually, it's useful work. Even bad reviews don't seem to do much in the way of permanent damage. The fact is, history is littered with bad reviews of writing we've come to regard as good work. Here are a few you might have missed...

A critic for *Contemporary Review* called Walt Whitman "incapable of true poetical originality" and James Russell Lowell wrote of Whitman's *Leaves of Grass*, "No, no, this kind of thing won't do..."

The critic John Dunlop considered *Gulliver's Travels*, "evidence of a diseased mind and a lacerated heart" and no less than Lord Byron wrote in a letter in 1814, "Shakespeare's name, you may depend on it, stands absurdly too high and will go down. He had no invention as to stories, none whatever. He took all his plots from old novels, and threw in their stories into a dramatic shape, at as little expense of thought as you or I could turn his plays back again into prose tales."

Walt Whitman, Jonathan Swift, William Shakespeare – all trashed by critics. So were Emily Bronte, Emily Dickinson, Lewis Carroll, and Mark Twain, to name only a few writers who actually did rather well for themselves.

Then there's the fact that many bad reviews are well-deserved. Nonetheless, authors of all kinds at least reserve the right to sit fuming over a bad review, sniffing, "and what books (movies, poems, plays, etc.) has *this* person ever written?" So, don't worry about the impact your review will have, just be as honest as possible about your reaction to the work, and write it as well as you can.

After all, writing criticism is a way to get published and for people to become acquainted with you as a writer. Editors are usually willing to consider a well-written review by someone who has actually read the book, seen the play, listened to the recording or concert, or sat through the film. The operative word of course is "well-written." It must be thoughtful, grasp the point, or note clearly the absence of a point.

What qualifies someone to be a critic? Training or education is helpful, but in real life the critic's main qualification is having his or her name after the word "by" on a review. Since many people loved work that a critic hated – or hated work a critic loved – so much for qualifications or being in touch with public tastes.

Online booksellers encourage people to post their opinions of books, thus, in effect, making everyone a critic, and it's kind of a nice way to start.

Writing is subjective – in the eye of the beholder. Jane Austen received some pretty awful reviews. So did Herman Melville, V. S. Naipaul, John Irving, Joyce Carol Oates, and nearly everyone else who has ever been published.

Tom Wolfe once wrote a scathing article attacking the work of Norman Mailer, John Irving, and John Updike because the three had all, in turn, written negatively about a book by Wolfe – a book that, incidentally, went on to become quite successful. So much for one man's – or three men's – opinions.

Some critics are taken to task for never writing bad reviews, as if that were a bad thing. Isn't it, after all, only another way of saying "if you can't say something nice, don't say anything at all?"

From a writer's perspective, reviews offer a world of opportunity. If you're writing the review, it's a chance to share your opinion while providing potentially useful information to your audience. Whether it's a book, movie, play, CD, or concert, you can help them to decide whether to seek it or avoid it – and why.

If it's your work that's getting reviewed, you can learn from the bad ones and read the good ones to your mother.

In a civilized world, everyone should be entitled to his or her opinion and those who choose to publish their opinions should be accorded a degree of respect, if not, perhaps, agreement.

The only way to learn to write is to write.
— **Peggy Teeters**

It is only one step from the sublime to the ridiculous.
— **Napoleon Bonaparte**

Nothing, not love, not greed, not passion or hatred, is stronger than a writer's need to change another writer's copy.
— **Arthur Evans**

The future belongs to those who believe in their dreams.
— **Eleanor Roosevelt**

A Writing Exercise

1. What was the book or film that left a lasting impression in your mind?

2. Write a 250-word piece on why it was good, why it was bad, and what single scenes or passages stood out or stayed with you.

3. Remember to follow the journalistic principles – whether the work you are describing is fiction or nonfiction – telling who, what, when, where, and why.

4. Can you make it better? If you loved it, can you make us all want to see it or read it. If you hated it, can you make us all feel like we should avoid that work like the proverbial plague.

Writing for Business...

... can be a big part of every writer's job – particularly if you decide to go into the business of writing. Because the fact is, businesses need a lot of writing. Some of it may not be the most exciting of tasks – does anyone read those annual reports or corporate brochures? But we keep the wheels of commerce turning and our checking accounts balanced with all kinds of business writing.

Another pleasant fact may emerge. Some business writing is pretty good. The weekly sizzle in *Business Week* and the *Economist*; *Forbes* and *Fortune* every two weeks; and the monthly interest in *Fast Company* and *Wired* can be a delight to read. Business writers Peter Drucker, Tom Peters, and Thomas Friedman, among others, have provided some of the most important writing on the economy. Though your initial business writing assignments likely won't be quite that exciting, it can be some of your most financially rewarding, particularly at the beginning of a writing career. Even though writing for business might not be on your short list of writing goals, it may well provide the income and experience that helps bring you closer to those goals.

Here are some of the types of business writing – a few we may cover in a bit more detail later on in this book:

- Advertising – we'll cover this in a bit;
- Annual Reports – a staple of the freelance writer's job. Too bad they're only needed once a year;
- Books – as more and more companies commission "corporate histories" or commemorative volumes, such as the visionary Chicago real estate developer who used his book as both a business gift and a promotional tool;
- Brochures;

- Collaterals – all the associated pieces (flyers, postcards, handbills, signage, sales sheets, buttons) used in selling;

- Feature Articles – placement in trade magazines;

- Grant-writing – critical to the many organizations (non-profits in particular) that are in the business of getting grants to remain in existence;

- Newsletters – basic communication tools of companies and associations for both internal and external distribution;

- Press Releases – the basic public relations vehicle, essential to any PR or marketing effort;

- RFP – a *Request for Proposal* directed to an advertising agency, PR firm, or other business entity, requires a written response that might determine future incomes or careers;

- 'Zines - (hey, I had to end the list with a "z" and e-magazines qualify.

Some of the writing that companies need can be dry. Some of the work, where you have to become expert in an area that, frankly, doesn't interest you all that much, can be tedious. But writers become writers to write and business writing is an area that can really generate satisfaction, while paying more than a few bills.

One 16-page brochure, for example, took a complex subject and put it into simple, conversational terms – something that accompanied every prospectus sent out to prospective investors. The brochure was titled *Understanding Options* and sought to explain the relationship of stock option contracts to stocks and their uses in combination in the investment markets.

In less than a year, more than 4 million copies of the brochure were distributed. For a writer, four million copies of anything is a pretty good number and the complex, technical subject suddenly seems a lot less boring.

Score one for simplified, readable writing for public communication.

A Writing Exercise

1. Choose a business subject that appears complicated to you, such as science, investing, or Greek tourism.

2. Find a book in a library or an article online dealing with that subject.

3. Read the introduction, preface, and/or the first chapter.

4. Now, returning to the library or online, find something on that subject with the words "understanding" or "simplified" or "made easy" as part of the title. Or perhaps something among the numerous books that list subjects followed by the lamentable words "for dummies" or "for idiots."

5. Read the introduction, preface or beginning chapter of that work.

6. Write a brief critical analysis of your examination of the technical or regular work compared to the more simplified version, noting if indeed the author had created a more understandable take on the subject and if, in your opinion, the process used would be transferable to other complex – or supposedly boring – subjects.

A Career Exercise

Are there any areas of business where you would like to become more knowledgeable? If so, start a "clip file" for each topic.

Have something to say, and say it as clearly as you can.
That is the only secret.

— **Matthew Arnold**

Write what you want to read. The person you know best in this world is you. Listen to yourself. If you are excited by what you are writing, you have a much better chance of putting that excitement over to a reader.

— **Robin McKinley**

Writing Speeches...

...is a fascinating area for a "hired writer" – a lot like being a ghost-writer, adopting the identity of someone else, writing in that person's voice, rarely having it known that the words being spoken are not those of the speaker, but of someone else. The speaker has control of the presentation and can influence audience mood and response. But the words, as they will be remembered, reported, and quoted are the substance of the speech.

The speechwriter for a public figure is writing both "for the record" and for history, hoping his or her words will resonate with constituents and be quoted as the basis of policy and informed opinion. For public relations professionals, speechwriting is one of many functions in which a writer presents a company or organization's positions in ways that could have major impact on stock prices, jobs, and possibly business sectors.

People often ask why so many speeches are boring, even when they are well rehearsed and delivered flawlessly from memory, like an actor delivering lines, rather than someone reading from a page being seen for the first time. Here's a possible explanation:

Sometimes a well-constructed speech, when it's read aloud, sounds like a well-constructed speech. A speechwriter will recognize immediately that is not a compliment. A speech should never sound as if it is being read – even when it's being read. Writing for the page is very different from the way most people actually speak. This is true whether the speaker is the president of a corporation or a bright young comedian appearing on stage for the first time.

Writing for the printed page requires a certain respect for basic rules of grammar, sentence structure, and paragraphs. The same is not true when speaking. A speech should sound as if it is part of a conversation the speaker is having with the audience. In conversation, even acknowledged masters of language rarely adhere rigidly to rules of grammar.

William F. Buckley, Jr., for example, a master of language skills with a vocabulary that would embarrass many thesaurus editors, would never sprinkle his written pages with "y'know" – most speakers' most overused device to keep the momentum of conversation moving forward and inviting listener agreement. The same Mr. Buckley, however, who in conversation routinely asks "how come," would always ask "why" in his written work.

"Uh" rarely appears in published writing. Someone in a written piece might say, "come over here and sit down with me," whereas a speaker might just as easily expand the invitation to, "Why don't you come and sit awhile" (leaving off the question mark). Never mind that the person hasn't indicated an unwillingness or a reason why he or she would not – which would justify the "why don't you…" prefix that is spoken countless times and goes unnoticed, as do all the uhs, y'knows, she says, he goes, I went, I'm like, and mmms that clutter most verbal exchanges.

President Ronald Reagan rarely began a sentence without first saying "Well…," followed by a pause. Some would say the use of "well…" was both a folksy colloquialism and a stalling device that allowed the president to delay his comment while he collected his thoughts.

Speakers should speak with feeling, with emotion, with heart. Good speechwriters, like ghostwriters, study their subjects carefully to get a feeling for their speech patterns, cadences, and what types of expressions or phrases would likely be used – or would never be used – by the speaker.

That seems fine. But all too often these same speechwriters go on to write the speeches in complete sentences, adjectives and adverbs neatly placed, never ending sentences with prepositions, and totally losing all sense of the feeling the speaker would likely convey if speaking extemporaneously. These writers probably even remember what a gerund is.

A favorite quote from Winston Churchill is not about blood, sweat and tears, but is his response to a woman who wrote to him, criticizing his colorful comments and frequent bad grammar when speaking in public. She reminded Mr. Churchill that he had a responsibility to set a good example for young people, if not for the entire nation.

Mr. Churchill's response was a simple, "Madam, this is the sort of nonsense up with which I will not put."

Speechwriters can make a poor speaker seem interesting and entertaining with facts, figures, anecdotes, humor, and content providing valuable information in interesting ways.

A good speech should have at least one "take-away" soundbite or quotable remark.

Speechwriters should study their speakers for cadence, lengths of sentences, slang usage, and where pauses fit best. They should also listen for the personal touches of color or habit that punctuate the speaker's most emotional, lively, or entertaining remarks and make a speech sound real... because real is almost never boring.

*My aim is to put down what I see and what I feel
in the best and simplest way I can tell it.*
— **Ernest Hemingway**

Writing is its own reward.
— **Henry Miller**

Tediousness is the most fatal of all faults.
— **Samuel Johnson**

A Writing Exercise

1. Speechwriting is about organization, pacing, timing, and content. Organize the speech as an opening, a presentation, and a closing.

2. Be aware of language. Speeches should sound like the speaker's voice and style, but should use words and terms easily understood by members of the audience, neither "talking up" to people or "down" to them.

3. The opening should include a greeting and an anecdote, constructed and delivered in a relaxed, friendly, conversational way, with an indication of what is to follow.

4. The presentation is the "body" of the speech. Its content should be largely constructed of short sentences with easily "processed" bites of information, allowing the audience time to digest what it hears.

5. Provide at least one good "take-away" – a useful, memorable fact. More than three such points could be too much. Don't overload an audience with information.

6. Direct people to sources for additional information on the subject, such as a Web site, article, or book.

7. Conclude with a brief summary of points covered, an expression of appreciation for the opportunity to speak, and thank the audience for its presence and attention.

8. Stay within the allotted time.

Writing a Particularly Important Speech…

…something that will be heard by important people and can have a major impact – can be tough on a writer. Knowing that the speech will be delivered on some momentous occasion before a huge audience and the memorable flowing words will not be credited to their true author can be hard to take. Some speechwriters in fact don't take it. David Frum writes books and makes frequent public appearances, never without being first introduced as "the man who inserted the phrase 'axis of evil' into one of President George W. Bush's most memorable State of the Union speeches. It was so memorable in fact that it was the "sound bite" – the phrase that made headlines the next day and is the only thing many people remember about the speech years later.

When a line – or a speech – gets such massive attention, it can be difficult for the writer not to jump up in the midst of the applause and shout, "I wrote that line!"

Most speechwriters resist the temptation, but it can be tough.

One of President Kennedy's close advisors was Theodore Sorensen, a man so close to Kennedy that he was said to be able to finish the president's sentences for him. The two men thought alike, which no doubt explains how Sorensen got the job and why he was so good at it. Critics insist that, "Ask not what your country can do for you; ask what you can do for your country," the most memorable and quoted passage of President Kennedy's inaugural address, was in fact written by Sorensen. The president denied it and so did Sorensen, yet the tale persists more than 40 years later.

The man the world knows as Mark Twain, the perpetually quotable writer of *The Adventures of Huckleberry Finn* and *Tom Sawyer*, was actually Samuel Clemens. In addition to his enduring personal fame and long list of accomplishments as the legendary Mr. Twain, he is widely credited with being the author and publisher of the *Personal Memoirs of Ulysses S. Grant*, one of the most popular books of the nineteenth century. It didn't matter that, as Twain, Mr. Clemens had enough fame to outlast generations of writers; he couldn't resist taking credit for a piece of writing that became such a huge success, much less allow credit to go to someone else – even if the someone else was the head of the country in which he lived.

Writing speeches or ghostwriting words to be attributed to someone else can pay very well, but a part of the fee is supposed to buy anonymity. When a work receives acclaim on a grand scale, the money suddenly becomes less important than receiving recognition for the something that achieves a level of success.

Comedy writers love hearing the laughs their words bring, but find the lack of recognition maddening. So very often, they try their hand at performing, with decidedly mixed results.

To a writer, the applause for the words is reward enough (though the payment for services is certainly a welcome addition to the applause). Knowing that the words were right and resonated with others, to be heard and remembered for untold days to come, is the job, even if credit is never accorded. It's the difference between being a writer and being a celebrity. History has shown, however, that when voices go silent and fame has faded, good writing lives on and the good writers know who wrote it.

A Writing Exercise

1. Think about speeches you've heard or read and consider why you remember them – what was it about the speech that makes you remember it.

2. Think of a well-known or classic song or a poem that best describes you or how you feel (Everything is Beautiful, Mr. Lonely, Someone to Watch Over Me, Stardust...). The words and verses are intended to evoke empathy, nostalgia or other feelings. Use them.

3. Write a one-page speech (250 words) describing how you feel about a particular subject in ways that will make others want to know more about you or the subject. Freely quote from poems or song lyrics that you believe describe how you feel or what you are like.

4. Try to adapt, modify, or substitute the lines taken from songs or poems, replacing them with original turns of phrase you think help express what you want to say.

5. Read what you've written, underlining a phrase or passage you think best describes what you want to say.

> *Writing gives you the illusion of control,*
> *and then you realize it's just an illusion,*
> *that people are going to bring their own stuff into it.*
> — **David Sedaris**

Writing Transitions…

…is about getting from one significant point to another without jarring the reader or interrupting the rhythm or flow of the written piece. It's what the writer Carroll Dale Short called, "the basic 'glue' of good writing."

Yet, transitions are an area of writing that frequently gets short-changed. In the grand scheme of outlining, plotting, conceptualizing, presenting, and telling the reader who, what, when, where, and why, transitions seem less important. They're not.

Sometimes it's simple. To some people, the conjunction "and" used at the beginning of a paragraph indicates a transition. And, in many cases, this is enough, though it's not the most creative or challenging approach to keeping the writing flowing. More sophisticated writers opt for words like "meanwhile" instead of "and," but that only adds more letters. It's just another shortcut, a functional tool.

Effective writing, writing that is remembered, underlined, highlighted, and sets a standard, does not rely on shortcuts. The writer takes us on a journey – the better the writing, the more interesting the journey.

A writer's transition can be smooth, artful, and deliberate. Or it can shock us a bit. It can offer some insight as it connects the scenes, or it can underline the thought that the character hasn't a clue. Connecting thoughts can be profound or prosaic. Just because something suggests an item is in addition to another item relating to the same subject does not make it a transition… unless, of course, it works. Good writers take us where they want us to go – and we enjoy the trip.

Different writing formats use different kinds of transitions. Transitions in fiction change the scene. In nonfiction, the transition might require a bit more attention. In essays or feature articles, the techniques are different. A section that begins with a phrase such as, "To put the subject in perspective," or, "At any rate…" lets the reader know the writer is shifting gears a bit and moving away from what has been presented so far – same subject, different direction.

Transitions are essential components of a written work, not just conjunctions seemingly thrown in as an afterthought. Without transitions, writing is just paragraphs strung together. Language provides words and phrases that serve as bridges to other words and phrases.

You may find writing transitions a bit different than the core of your work. For example, a cliché can be an excellent transition, taking readers to familiar, often neutral territory, whereas you might not want to use that construction in a key part of your work. Most good writing treats a cliché like the flu – turn away from it, avoid it, if possible take a vaccine to prevent it. On the other hand, the reason we tell you to avoid using clichés is that many have been so overused that their very presence undermines a thoughtful, well constructed, or creative body of writing. The phrases, "But, at the end of the day," "Let's cut to the chase," "The bottom line," or other such tired lines may seem out of place on an otherwise thoughtful page. Going between thoughts, well, that might be something else.

In proposals or important presentations, where being concise, unique or imaginative can determine success or failure, a cliché or a simple transitional device can often take the reader where they need to go with great efficiency.

It has been said that half of learning is reminding ourselves of what we already know.

For example, (pause). Ha! There's a familiar enough phrase and a very concise and effective transition. Now we can move on to something else. And another thing...

A Writing Exercise

1. Choose a lengthy story in a current newspaper. Note the writer's transitions from one section of the story to another.

2. Choose a piece of fiction writing and note transitions from scenes to chapters or from one chapter to another.

3. Note at least three passages in which you think the transitions could be handled differently or improved.

The act of writing is an act of optimism. You would not take the trouble to do it if you felt it didn't matter.
— **Edward Albee**

Writing Adjectives...

...might seem to be something you've been doing ever since you learned to write. Yet, understanding the real power of certain words – or what I call the *Successful Adjective* – is something writers learn to appreciate, particularly writers in the public relations field. For most writing, choosing the correct adjective can bring color, energy, exuberance, clarity, or specific details to a subject. For ad writers and PR professionals, however, adjectives can define, promote, or even change a reader's opinion. And, correctly used over time, they add value. Think of Volvo and the simple adjective "safe." Simply put, it's taking the time to go from choosing a good word to using *exactly the right word.* Consider the word *success.*

What makes something successful? How is success expressed? Superior sales, public acceptance, a long record of profit and growth, or general agreement? *Sometimes the determinant is someone simply describing something verbally or in writing as "successful."* That can be all it takes if the description and/or the source of the designation has credibility – and credibility itself is an often subjective term. Sometimes even a non-credible source can determine status or quality if that source is quoted or repeated often enough. Hearing something said or seeing it written numerous times doesn't necessarily make it true, but it can help make it appear to be true – to be common knowledge or the conventional wisdom or simply a reflection of what most people think they have heard or know.

When a writer or speaker describes a subject, a book, or a film, for example, as being successful or very successful or *highly* successful and no one rises to challenge the claim or ask for documentation or a source, the description is likely to stand but, more importantly, to be repeated – picked up by other writers and used by them, reinforcing the original reference. If the audience assumes the writer or speaker to be credible, which is generally the case, the designation of "successful" not only applies, but stands.

An exception to this – or, more correctly, the semi-exception – is in politics, where lines are drawn and the designation of a "credible source" is in the eye of the beholder and only accorded those of one's own party, philosophy, or tribe. That opponents lack credibility is both a stated and an assumed truth, again, with no validation required.

In religion, where much depends on faith, interpretation becomes truth and that truth is to be accepted without challenge. A famous line directed to skeptics is, "to those who believe, no explanation is necessary; to those who do not believe, no explanation will suffice."

So, is it possible then to just declare something to be successful, hot, the people's choice, the leading brand, the most popular anything, the fastest-selling something, on the cutting edge, or the new paradigm, and have everyone believe it just because it is written or said in public?

Until it is challenged by someone with a larger pen or pulpit, long answer is *yes*. In news writing or press releases, adjectives need to be used more cautiously. An ad writer or the originator of collateral materials, such as brochures or corporate profiles can call a product or a company "dynamic" or "exciting" or "superior" or "innovative" or groundbreaking" or "fantastic" but such subjective terms lack the objectivity a writer or reporter can use in describing a subject. The same rule applies to editors or producers in determining the credibility or value of a news release.

The editor or writer, in the latter cases, needs to produce and judge something objectively and based on the facts. Descriptive is okay, but the adjectives in such cases are the responses and opinions determined by the reader.

A Writing Exercise

1. Choose a piece of writing in a newspaper or a magazine.

2. Highlight or circle the adjectives used in the piece.

3. Consider if the adjectives show a bias for or against the subject or some other part of the story.

4. Determine if the quality of the piece would have been improved, diminished, or otherwise altered if the adjectives were deleted or different.

5. Choose a commercial product or service that you're familiar with. Spend a bit of time thinking about what specific adjective connected to that product will make it more memorable. What adjective lies at the soul of this product? (Note: it may not be totally profound or surprising, but it should be appropriate. Also, you may manufacture something. (Volvos are "safe." BMWs are "ultimate." Popeyes Chicken is "spicy." KFC is "finger-lickin' good." Get it?)

6. Once you've determined the adjective, see if you can't create some sort of public relations top-spin. A Volvo book on safe driving. BMW sponsoring the Ultimate Road Rally. Or Popeyes naming the Top Ten Spicy Personalities.

Writing a Book Proposal...

...is sort of like handwriting. In elementary school everyone learned the same letters and how they should be written. But somewhere along the way, some handwriting became so sloppy that hardly anyone could make out what it was the writer was trying to say. Meanwhile, others maintained handwriting that was clear and easy to follow. Still others wrote the letter "f" so that it looked like the number seven.

Well not every writer wants to write a book, so why be concerned about writing book proposals? The answer is much of life is about proposals, from new business pitches to requests for funding to résumés addressing the reader's question, "why should I choose you or what you have to offer?" And, of course, "will you marry me?"

The concept and focus is much the same, though the formats may vary.

Here's the generally agreed upon format for a book proposal:

1. Title Page. This would contain the name of the book, your byline, the book's category – as in fiction, nonfiction, poetry, memoir, biography, etc. – and how to contact you;

2. Synopsis. A one- or two-page explanation of what the book is about;

3. Outline. A general outline that could resemble a table of contents and lays out the format and order in which the material will be presented;

4. Target Audience. A paragraph or two under the heading "target audience" tells who will want to buy this book, estimating the audience size in numbers and, if applicable,

professions and titles (such as teachers, corporate CEOs, custodians, cartoonists, lawyers, pastry chefs, Mafia hit men, etc);

5. The Competition. Next, write a paragraph under the heading "the competition" and list books that are similar or try to make the same case, and tell why yours is better. If there is nothing out there like what you have, say that.

6. Author Bio. Include a double-spaced one-page bio (not a résumé – think of the space on the book jacket under "about the author") that tells the editor why you are qualified to write this book, noting your professional experience or connection to the material.

7. A Sample. Include a sample introduction and/or a sample chapter.

There's an old adage that everyone has a book in him (or her). It's probably true. But that doesn't mean the prospective author has a winning proposal in them, or that, once published, the book would be all that readable. The simple truth is that every life is a story and we all have something to say. That can include the "life" of a business, a particularly interesting campaign for dog catcher (or some other political office), or something in which you have a special interest or expertise (Diet Soft Drinks and The People Who Love Them Too Much). To get that story to others, an editor or publisher wants to see a proposal explaining why what you are proposing is worthy of publication, who will buy it, and why you should be the one to write it.

If you'd like to know more, there are books that tell you *How to Write a Book Proposal* and other books that tell you *How to Write Book Proposals That Sell*. What they should all be called is *How to Write a Book Proposal The Way the Author of This Book Writes a Book Proposal*, since there is actually no one way to do it, much less a guarantee that the proposal will succeed.

But, considering how much it takes to write a book, you might want to develop your proposal writing skills along the way.

A few more notes on proposals from this author. Different editors and agents have their own ideas about what they like to see in proposals. One "how to" article noted a completed proposal should be about 80 pages in length. Most writers would choke upon hearing this… including me. Occasionally, word of this approach reaches publishers… and they begin choking, as well. Eventually, we stop choking long enough to agree this is not good advice to give prospective authors.

"I have entire books that are only 80 pages long," one editor noted, intent on having the final word.

My first published book was the result of a letter and a two-page outline. My second book followed an idea that was pitched in a phone conversation. Sometimes that's all it takes.

If your concept is clear enough, the contents can be described concisely and, if the editor already knows the writer, his or her research methods, writing style and ability to deliver, pages of explanation are unnecessary.

Editors often require that for novels and poetry, an entire completed manuscript be submitted, along with a brief synopsis of the work, before a deal is made, unless author and publisher have an established relationship, in which case, the deal is made on promises and trust. And, that said, unless you're already famous, if you've got a first novel or a book of poetry, look into some sort of self-publishing, publishing on demand, or publishing house that specializes in "vanity." You'll pay – but you'll have a book, and, if it gets read and reviewed, publishers will become interested.

For a nonfiction book, this is something entirely different. Editors want the author to not only clearly present the idea of the book, but provide additional information that makes a case for why it should be published. Think Target Audience and Marketing. Publishers are keenly interested in selling the books they publish. If you can make a case, it can happen. Remember, every author was once a first-time author.

Think seriously about how your book would be marketed and who would buy it (that Target Audience section is critical). Anticipate what questions an editor is likely to ask about the project when you pitch your idea and answer those questions in your submission.

Proposals for great books are often rejected many times before finding a publisher. There is actually a book of collected rejection letters to Herman Melville, Jack London, Henry James, Ernest Hemingway, Norman Mailer, Gertrude Stein, James Joyce, Agatha Christie, Mary Higgins Clark, Vladimir Nabokov, and some other folks who subsequently managed to find editors and publishers who appreciated their work.

Editors, assistant editors, and the readers who work for assistant editors are subjective readers like anyone else and their opinions are not necessarily an indication of quality. (As a young editor, Michael Korda recommended to his employers at Simon & Schuster that the company publish a book called *The Catcher in the Rye* by J.D. Salinger. His employers passed on the project, editors at Little, Brown & Company did not, and the book hasn't been out of print since 1951).

Buy a lot of stamps and don't be discouraged if you have to use them all. Most writers do.

Ability is nothing without opportunity.
— **Napoleon Bonaparte**

A Writing Exercise

1. Write a sample book proposal. This can be fun. Either take some idea you already have (most writers do) and put it into a proposal, or look at the marketplace for books and see if you can find a potentially popular niche. (A friend who publishes books on advertising keeps threatening to write "Your Cat's Favorite Commercials." So far, we've been spared.)

2. Choose a favorite book and "unwrite" it. That is, go backwards from the finished work, deconstruct it, and see what it would look like as a proposal. This completed exercise should produce the nucleus of a book proposal. You need to identify and then write:

- Title Page. Do this in the proposal format.
- Synopsis. Briefly, tell us what it's about. Sell us the book – tell us what you consider to be the strongest, most important, memorable, or valuable points in the book – for readers, the "take-aways."
- Outline. Briefly, outline the book.
- Target Audience. Tell us who the book appeals to most (primary target market). You might also indicate what additional individuals or groups might be interested (secondary Target market)
- The Competition. What other well known books have been written on the same subject. Tell us why this book is different from other books on the subject and will sell better.
- Author Bio. What specifically qualified this author to do it well.

Writing Fiction...

As the author of more than a dozen nonfiction books, I have often wondered about fiction – my own, that of the writers I love to read, and especially those writers whose writing I hate – what is the point of it?

There is so much heavy, serious business in the world, so much to do and so much to occupy our conscious moments... why fiction? There are needs to be met, like food and rent and paying bills. So why make up stories for which some people are paid nothing and others are paid huge amounts – stories about, with all due respect to John Irving and Thomas Harris, bears riding unicycles or a brilliant psychiatrist who is also a cannibal and serial killer? Is such writing contributing something to our base of human knowledge?

Many scholars regard a great deal of fiction as literature, while others simply call it "entertainment" – although I have often questioned the sanity of people who are entertained by cannibal stories or pretty much any story that would prompt a reviewer to describe it as "deeply disturbing." Even more, the screen adaptation with the line in the ad that promises it will shock and disturb you. The inclusion of this phrase is aimed at bringing people into the theaters.

As with roller coasters, I've never understood why people pay to experience – even second-hand – the feelings of terror, shock, torture, cruelty, and the bloody nightmares that they try to avoid in reality all their lives. Yet, be it Bram Stoker or Stephen King, the horror genre has a devoted audience.

But Stephen King notwithstanding, can writers justify making up stories as a real job or expect to make a living from it?

A psychologist might say to induce certain emotions is mentally healthy. A comic novel is a series of jokes or funny experiences and we know laughter has been scientifically proven to be good for us. In that same vein, erotic writing, adventures, and even horror may help provide insight, information, or understanding about ourselves and others.

Fiction is, in fact, important on many levels, from being a form of expression to an area of escape to a means of *expanding one's mind*. Storytelling may conform to journalistic principles of telling readers who, what, when, where, why, and how, but it also asks *what if…* and *what then?* The challenge for a writer to create people, places, and things that are fantastic, outrageous, richly or bleakly presented in ways that allow readers to imagine or believe the impossible is possible, requires the writer to go beyond *prescribed limits of descriptive journalism to see not only what is, but what could be.* The result of the exercise for the writer is a greater understanding of deeper, lighter, darker, and richer techniques for presenting material.

When I have written my best fiction, I made friends of the characters I created. They were as real in my mind as my memories of actual experiences with my family and friends. True, I could control them – even kill them off if I chose to – but a writer first asks in such cases, *is that really what the character would do?* And in answering that question, the character becomes a real virtual person, independent of the writer.

We can affect our spaces – the New York of Woody Allen's *Manhattan* is not the New York of Martin Scorsese's *Mean Streets*. We can create our versions of places and people, sad and funny, wonderful or terrible, serene or chaotic. We can go alone or with friends. We can take our readers on journeys that show them a war from the battlefield or a star from the other side.

I was sorry when that fascinating Mr. Gatsby was shot. And in his swimming pool yet. But could that story have ended another way and still held up so many years later? And Juliet and her Romeo – what a sad series of misunderstandings, but could anyone imagine them growing old together and living happily ever after? And what Dorothy learned about life and herself and getting along with others on that one brief visit to Oz is more than some people learn in a lifetime.

To create and to express is great to experience, even if the experience is only vicarious or virtual.

So would we all have been better off if the people whose day job is making up stories had done something else – something more sensible, more grown up? Probably not.

Fiction is writing the human condition, who we are, why we act this way, why we think others act the way they do…

For all the bad books and plays and scripts and poems, there was someone who put ink to paper with the thought that he or she wanted to say something, do something, to share something. Those are very good reasons to write fiction.

Perhaps it would be better not to be a writer, but if you must, then write. If all feels hopeless, if that famous 'inspiration' will not come, write. If you are a genius, you'll make your own rules, but if not - and the odds are against it - go to your desk no matter what your mood, face the icy challenge of the paper – write.
— **J. B. Priestly**

A Writing Exercise

1. Write a page of fiction in third-person voice. Be the storyteller – the unseen observer of events. Tell a story.

2. For inspiration, draw from your own experience: begin with an incident that happened to you in your life (a vacation, a job, a party, an unusual friend…).

3. After setting up your premise, stop relating the facts of the story and ask yourself, "what if…?" Imagine something happening in your story, or to your people, that did not actually happen, but might have happened if circumstances had been different.

4. Experiment with a few different possibilities.

The story… must be a conflict, and specifically, a conflict between the forces of good and evil within a single person.
— **Maxwell Anderson**

To most readers the word 'fiction' is an utter fraud. They are entirely convinced that each character has an exact counterpart in real life and that any small discrepancy with that counterpart is a simple error on the author's part. Consequently, they are totally at a loss if anything essential is altered. Make Abraham Lincoln a dentist, put the Gettysburg Address on his tongue, and nobody will recognize it.
— **Louis Auchincloss**

Writing in a Journal...

...is something writers are often advised to do as they head down the literary road. Many, if not most, do begin a journal – usually the men are more self-conscious about it than the women – but few keep it up. It's not unusual for that journal to be abandoned after a few entries.

There are several likely reasons for this. First and not least is that it is a good bit of work – it's a time commitment and most people feel that they're already over-committed. The notion that what free time can be choked out of a schedule should go to what some feel is a form of "homework" just isn't motivating enough.

Others start by making intricate entries – as if their journals were a ship's log of their life, with each minute and every minor errand accounted for so that it can be filed and reviewed by some high controlling authority at a later date. Still others worry that if they note their most personal and private thoughts and activities in their journals, someone might find the journals and read what could be embarrassing or incriminating information, as if it is inevitable that everyone will, at some point in his or her life, get around to committing a murder or embezzling huge sums of money from their companies, or engaging in the type of stock fraud that sent Martha Stewart up the river without a frying pan. Or perhaps one will become involved in a romantic affair of scandalous proportions, and the revelations in the journal will be found on the front page of the *National Enquirer*. Certainly such exposure could be devastating – destroying innocent people's lives! So, be safe. Why start a journal? As if.

The journal is usually abandoned early on simply because it becomes a chore, easily skipped when its keeper feels too tired to complete an entry or becomes engaged in something much more interesting, such as the activities listed above.

That's dumb. Here are some words to the wise that may help you get started on a journal that not only helps you become a better writer, but ends up being a document that you can actually share parts of.

First, keeping a journal is a way writers (and non-writers) can note ideas or observations that might be useful at a later time, and might otherwise be forgotten. So, brief jottings of observations – or the beginnings of an idea – will go nicely in that journal you keep handy.

If you wish, you can use the journal as a substitute for therapy. It certainly costs less, and, for some, it can be a lifeline, serving a therapeutic function, a place to unload troubling private thoughts or fears or fantasies. It can be cathartic. It can be the most non-judgmental place to be as expressive, outrageous – more unlike one's self than a person was ever believed to be – or gentle, senti-mental, romantic, irreverent, bold, or all of the above in one para-graph. No one will "grade" or review or even see a single entry or the entire body of writing, unless the author allows it. Confiding such information in a friend or family member has been known to come back to bite a person, should that particular relationship encounter rough times.

If you'd feel more comfortable with less personal revelations in your journal, how about observations on the passing scene? Whether it is how people behave at a coffee bar, your take on the latest political dust-up, or surreal ruminations (you know if we really did train penguins as waiters, it could start a trend. Par-rots at the drive-in, taking your order, "Awk, value meal number two!") You'll be exercising those writing muscles and having a bit of fun.

Your journal can be as totally private or as open as you choose it to be. It can include phone numbers, recipes, test scores, jokes, favorite memories, and sketches. There are no rules. Busy people who are convinced they don't have time to write a journal entry each day, can write in it once a week or once a month or as sporadically as they choose.

For people who do write a journal page or more a day, it can be not only a form of therapy, but a way to get into a habit of writing down thoughts, quotes, titles, ideas, or other bits and pieces of life matter – silly or sensational – on a fairly regular basis.

Journals come in a variety of shapes and sizes and colors with leather bindings or slashes of color. They're at bookstores, card shops, drug stores, or flea markets. They don't have to be fancy – unless of course you're someone who insists that your innermost thoughts and random jottings can only travel first class. In such cases, the high-end leather with thick pages and fine binding is a great place to hold your best mental pictures and phrases.

Find a blank book that feels good and smells good. One that's easily portable, or one that will be a welcome sight at the end of a day. Or at the start of a day. Or two-thirds of the way through a day. Whenever. The key is when it's the time the writer feels like writing, that's the time you'll be glad you now have the habit of jotting things down in a journal.

Your journal is about you, to you, for you – test yourself, judge yourself, make mistakes… and get in the habit of writing.

The journal is a tool; a place to park an idea for a story or a plan for a party or to give tangible form to a dream to be remembered. It's a place where you can be yourself – or someone else. It's a place where you can share secrets and truth or make up lies.

Whatever… it's between you and the book.

A Writing Exercise

1. Acquire a blank book of bound pages – thick or thin, spiral-bound, glued, or saddle-stitched.

2. Use it as a journal. Make entries in it over the course of two weeks. The length of each entry and how often you make them is up to you. But take it seriously.

3. At the end of the two week period, review what you've written. See how the journal works for you. Make some notes on the pages. Underline what you believe are points worth noting and remembering, and, perhaps, could be the topic for a few more journal entries.

Hopefully, at the end of the two-week period you will choose to continue keeping a journal (even if it's not required by a teacher or mentor) and come to regard it as the useful tool it can be.

I have been successful probably because I have always realized that I knew nothing about writing and have merely tried to tell an interesting story entertainingly.
— **Edgar Rice Burroughs**

Everybody walks past a thousand story ideas every day. The good writers are the ones who see five or six of them. Most people don't see any.
— **Orson Scott Card**

It is perfectly okay to write garbage – as long as you edit brilliantly.
— **C. J. Cherryh**

Writing Something Funny...

...writers soon learn, is serious business. As with any type of writing, the end result is always very subjective – with humor, perhaps more subjective than most. Creativity and language skills are important factors, but incorporating comedic touches requires added dimensions of both. Paradoxically, humor is serious business. Expectations are high, wide, and diverse. Laughter might be, as the adage suggests, universal, but writing something that's funny can be quite a challenge.

So how does one write comedy, whether for a film, a play, a story, an act, an opening "icebreaker" line in a speech, or an ad that's due tomorrow? We'll start by saying there is no single answer and then move on to try to give you a few hints.

Woody Allen is credited with the explanation that comedy is tragedy plus time – meaning that some events that are considered tragic, shocking, and/or painful at the time they occur are good subjects for funny remarks after a period of time has passed. That's kind of useful. One type of comedy uses what is known as "the disaster effect." The shock that something could go truly wrong, and the relief that it didn't. The slip on the banana peel. All things considered, there could be a broken bone or a serious head injury, but, instead, it was just a pratfall and no harm done. All of this happens in an instant and we laugh. OK, so "the disaster effect" is one type of humor.

Here are a few more hints, served up by my good friend Bruce Bendinger in his classic copywriting book, *The Copy Workshop Workbook*. He called it, "Ha! A Quick Course in Comedy."

There is usually some sort of contrast or conflict that is resolved in a surprising way. That surprise makes us laugh.

Some of the devices are:

- **The Double Meaning.** The internal tension of the double meaning generates the humor.

- **Exaggeration.** Taking some aspect to a humorous extreme can often get a laugh. Treating something big as being small – in an ironic way – is kind of exaggeration in reverse. "Slapstick" is very broad comedy. It's exaggeration in action.

- **Incongruity.** Total surprise. Something from out of left field.

- **Humanity.** Often, the humor comes from something we recognize: the wisdom/innocence of a child; the irreverence you often find in older people who truly have "been there done that;" the mother-in-law.

Also, there are formats, the light bulb joke, country humor, the blonde joke, and so on.

And, of course, other variations. For example, the running gag, which, hopefully, gets funnier as it gets repeated. Rodney Dangerfield's line, "I don't get no respect," was a good example. The line itself is not all that funny, but with his delivery and in the context of other gags and stories, it works. And that's part of the trick. As we've all experienced, some people can tell a joke, or deliver a line, or tell a story better than others.

Doing this well isn't simple, there is a whole list of related issues. Timing, for example. The right or wrong timing can make or break a joke or bit of humor. But the goal is simple – getting a laugh – or a chuckle – whatever is the desired response from your audience.

Think of these devices and formats as lenses. Just like a magnifying glass or a fun house mirror, take a look at a topic through these lenses and you just might be able to write something funny.

A Writing Exercise

1. Find examples of four types of humor: a one-liner, an anecdote, a lunch or dinner speaker's opening "icebreaker" joke, and a "visual" attempt at humor in an ad.

2. Consider the source and structure of the humor and why people might find it funny or not funny – a good-natured insult, a "fish out of water" story, something self-deprecating, an ability of anyone or everyone to relate, etc.

3. Pick a topic. Now look at the four humor categories: Double Meaning, Exaggeration, Incongruity, and Humanity. Now see if you can write the beginnings of a joke in each category. You might be surprised. See if you can get something going with humor categories: light bulb jokes, blonde jokes, etc.

4. Now, start with a target audience. Using the same four categories, try to write a humorous bit that relates to that particular audience. You'll see how the "know your audience" rule is particularly important when trying to write something funny.

Writing Poetry...

...is one of the most difficult types of writing. Or perhaps it's the least difficult. Consider Shakespeare, Wordsworth, Whitman, Shelley, and Keats. Great poets. Everyone seems to agree.

And there are others: Dorothy Parker, Jimmy Carter, Paul McCartney, Lawrence Ferlinghetti, and Rod McKuen. Regarding their poetry... not quite everyone agrees. So how do we know who is truly a great or even a good poet? The answer? You decide. You get to make that determination. Poetry is probably the most subjective kind of writing. And, as we've noted repeatedly, judging most writing is a subjective process at best. Who should be permitted to judge what is "good" in so creative and emotionally expressive a literary form?

There are poetry writing courses where one can receive a presumably enlightened overview and explanation of verse, iambic pentameter, the troche, the anapest, the dactyl, the amphibrach, the spondee, ideas, rhymes, and reflections, as well as dark or gothic, religious, or romantic, erotic imagery, or what is a descriptive poem or narrative or dramatic or didactic poetry or light verse.

Yet, the uniqueness and individualism that characterizes the genre as a form can perhaps only be judged as bad when it is clearly derivative or evocative of something that negates that individualism or originality.

Whether lyrical, coarse, brooding, romantic to the point of sappiness, or drenched in symbolism, humor or allusion, good and bad in poetry is very much in the eye and ear of the beholder.

Robert Frost spoke a poem of his for President John F. Kennedy's inauguration; Maya Angelou read one of hers at the inauguration of President Bill Clinton. Some people loved one or both, others did not. Either way, both are now part of American history.

Great Britain has long had a national poet – a poet laureate – whose job is to compose official poetry for such occasions as the king's and queen's birthday, coronations, weddings and births in the royal family, and to commemorate great victories in war. Chaucer, Wordsworth, and Tennyson all held the job at various times.

The poet laureate position in the United States first came into being in 1985, and Robert Penn Warren was appointed to the post a year later. Warren was also a novelist and literary critic, remembered for his novel *All the King's Men*, but it is his poetry that won him the coveted Pulitzer Prize. Twice.

There is no comparable position to poet laureate for other types of writers. There is no novelist laureate or cookbook author laureate or sports writer laureate, no designated official national writer of "how-to" books in either the U.S. or Britain. We had "beat poets" in coffee houses around the world, expressing the mood of a new generation, and then came the "poetry slams" – a sort of comedy club for aspiring poets. While it might not be for everyone, the form in all its variations has survived the centuries.

Maybe one reason many people find poetry difficult to appreciate is because some poems rhyme and others don't. Some are very serious; others not so. As the language experts say, either is correct.

A poem can be romantic or wistful or funny or dark or heavy. It can serve to make a point in ways simple or profound; deep or wistful. Politicians love quoting poetry and one can only wonder, after hearing the quote inserted by a speechwriter, if the politician knows the rest of the poem or only the quote.

Advertisers include poetic verse to help create a mood or tone for their messages. Many of us use the great poets' words to emphasize a point or express a sentiment that is deep in our hearts, even if someone else expressed it first...

The World Is Too Much with Us…
A thing of beauty is a joy forever…
Shall I compare thee to a summer's day?
Beauty is truth, truth beauty…
When I am old, I shall wear purple…
Once upon a midnight dreary, while I pondered weak and weary…
Ships that pass in the night…
And miles to go before I sleep.

Some men need to stress that they are not much for poetry, suggesting it's a woman's game. Maybe. But maybe, like Jimmy Carter and Paul McCartney, there are men who feel very strongly that expressing their innermost emotions does not make them any less men. But poets may be the greatest risk-takers among all writers, exposing the most private, sentimental thoughts, prayers, dreams, hopes, and fears – talking to themselves, to those they love, and to God. Out loud.

The last two lines of Robert Browning's poem from *Pippa Passes* have been quoted with some frequency for nearly 150 years…

The year's at the spring;
The day's at the morn;
Morning's at seven;
The hill-side's dew-pearled;
The lark's on the wing;
The snail's on the thorn:
God's in his heaven…
All's right with the world!

John Milton's *Paradise Lost*, written around 1665, ends with the words:

They, hand in hand, with wandering steps and slow,
Through Eden took their solitary way.

Fortunately, poets have continued to do so ever since.

A Writing Exercise

1. Examine the writing of three poets from three different periods.

2. Choose three poems – one from each poet.

3. Write a one paragraph analysis of the point of the poem – what the poet was trying to say – and if, in your opinion, the objective was achieved or what you found lacking in the manner it was presented.

Next to doing things that deserve to be written,
nothing gets a man more credit, or gives him more pleasure
than to write things that deserve to be read.
— Lord Chesterfield

Writing Memoirs...

...was once considered a category reserved for old retired politicians, statesmen, people who achieved something great, and aging movie stars (think Winston Churchill, Dwight Eisenhower, Charles Lindbergh, Joan Crawford, or Bette Davis). Then came *Angela's Ashes*, Frank McCourt's memoir of his sainted mother and a childhood spent in poverty in his beloved Ireland. Several million hardcover copies later, the memoir was repositioned and so sought-after a form by mainstream publishers that old Indians, old soldiers, middle-aged executives, any young women who ever appeared on a TV game show, and 15 year-old rock stars were telling their stories to tape recorders and signing the finished products at Barnes & Noble a few months later.

Some writers are dismissive of the form, believing that people who write memoirs are not writers at all, but simply storytellers in possession of extraordinarily large egos. At least they are not "serious writers," they sniff. Real writers, tradition demands, write about subjects other than themselves. In addition, many see the memoir as seed material to be adapted and exaggerated to become fiction, possibly a screen play of the "based on a true story" category. My own opinion - I think this growth of the memoir genre is good news.

Times change. The memoir is no longer merely the genre of the old and accomplished, or the simply vain. According to Joyce Maynard, the memoir – factual or fictionalized – has become, at least momentarily, the book genre du jour. And, I guess as long as we have memories, we have a memoir in each of us. I think this is a good thing.

It makes sense when you think about it. After all, isn't the age-old advice to writers, "write what you know?" In the memoir, we are each of us the ultimate expert, and we can take that wherever we want. We can use those writing personal experiences as the inspiration for fiction as well as nonfiction.

I know that this has its elements of controversy among purists, but as a launching pad for writers, the advantages outweigh the criticisms.

In her book, *The Forest for the Trees*, Betsy Lerner writes about the reactions people have to reading stories written by people they know, as in celebrities – wondering who the inspiration was for that character or who this person is supposed to be. People read their own feelings into books, assuming certain works of fiction simply had to be based on truth or are merely thinly disguised autobiographies. Sometimes they are.

But, then again, projecting assumptions and misreading facts not in evidence can also extend to nonfiction. As the line goes, "it's always something." A story from a friend of mine, who had a number of books published: This writer had not been in touch with someone in more than a decade. When they finally did see each other after that long absence, the writer asked the friend if he had read any of his (the writer's) books. The friend's reply was that he remembered the writer's first book well, as it was based on an idea stolen from him, for which he'd never gotten credit. It was one of the very rare occasions the writer remembered being left speechless. He had no idea what the friend was talking about and doesn't to this day.

The lesson? People don't always read what the writer writes. And that subjective thing I keep talking about? When you show people the world from your perspective, you get to see how many different ways other people see things. It may or may not be common to read things that are not there or assume a piece of writing was inspired by something it was not. Think of it as an additional opportunity for surprising and enriching experiences.

If it is true that everyone has a story to tell or that everyone has one good book somewhere deep within (though many people don't happen to believe that is the case), then the memoir or the memoir-as-inspiration-for-fiction can be that book. Once it was accepted that in order to publish a memoir the writer had to be someone famous or have experienced something unusual or amazing, but today that is less the case – if it's the case at all.

Just because the memoir makes it a better world for writers, doesn't mean it's a better world for readers. A person who does well in the stock market or loses a bundle at poker or who had an affair with anyone – famous or not – or saved the life of a fireman or had a relative or a pet die at a young age, can be the author of a published memoir today.

Amber Fry told her story of carrying on a romance with a man later convicted of killing his wife. Did people really want to know what it was like for her growing up or if she's on good terms with her parents? A writer related the tale, allegedly in Ms. Fry's own words and it became a national best-selling book, with screen rights sold to a movie producer. More serious books by writers are on the table at the book store, under a sign reading "any three titles – 99 cents."

A value of memoir writing, even for a young person, is that it represents an exercise in storytelling, whether romanticized, exaggerated, funny, or hard-edged. It is also a journalistic exercise in that a memoir would follow the principles of including who, what, when, where, why, and how. And one more valuable possibility that must be mentioned – the older people in your life. Grandparents, aunts, and uncles. My guess is many of them have a story worth telling and a story worth sharing – even if only with others in your family. You might want to wait until your own memoir has a few more chapters, but why not start by helping others in your family with theirs. It's great writing exercise for you – to help put that life story into something others will enjoy reading and what a wonderful gift you will be giving your own family – a bit of history they can share.

We'll set aside the epic question of why one memoir or other story, true or false, is more worthy of publication than another. The simple answer is because the editor or publisher liked it. Or, if it's a "vanity" publication, simply because someone wrote the check. But, in the case of family members you care about, the point is to write it down before those memories are lost. All things considered, the world will probably be a better place if you give it one more memoir.

Have something to say, and say it as clearly as you can.
That is the only secret.
— **Matthew Arnold**

The act of writing is an act of optimism. You would not take the trouble to do it if you felt it didn't matter.
— **Edward Albee**

All writing is a process of elimination.
— **Martha Albrand**

A Writing Exercise

1. A memoir is not an autobiography, in that the former is a re-membrance of only an incident, experience, or part of a life, while the latter is a recounting of the whole life.

2. Choose an incident from your life.

3. List who, what, when, where, why, and how facts relating to that incident.

4. Develop the facts into a brief (750 words or less) first-person narrative... a memoir.

5. The Family Memoir. Make a list of some of the older members of your family. Add to that other older people you might know – family, friends, etc. See what stories they might have – war veter-ans, people coming here from overseas, a Peace Corps adventure, college pranks... If you're so inclined, start on a memoir project. Get a tape recorder and schedule a sit-down visit. You may be surprised at what just one session will generate.

Writing Newsletters...

...may have a decidedly unexciting ring to some people. Yet, it's one of the best ways for a young writer to get started – and get paid. And even in this high-tech twenty-first century, they need to be written. Perhaps posted on a Web site – or e-mailed to a customer list – or even printed on an actual piece of paper with the not insignificant investment of a postage stamp. Today, more than ever, companies have to stay in touch with their customer base and newsletters are still a great way to do it. Though technology has added some interesting topspin.

Today, your electronic e-mail can have imbedded video – nothing like a dancing hamster to pep up the letterhead. We can integrate little bits of database. (How's your Rottweiler Fluffy, and is that left-handed nail file working out?) We can add links, and animations, and if it's computer-based, it can be in color for no extra charge. Best of all, we can look better than ever. Most graphics programs have some templates that are quite nice – and we can find more templates for not a lot of money – so we're not necessarily stuck with our own clumsy attempts at design. Mastheads, font decisions, and graphic grids have all been worked out. And we can do our jobs and write the darn thing.

Certainly the world is full of many second-rate newsletters. After all, when you think of it, half the newsletters in the world are below average. But... you have a first-rate chance to make yours interesting, readable, and a useful sample in your growing portfolio of writing you've done. As your career grows, it may be that the newsletters, catalogs, and brochures that make up so much of a working writers job history, end up in the seconds pile with just a few superb examples left, but even when those newsletters are thinly-disguised direct mail pieces, reworked sections of promotional literature, or excerpts from previously published work, they are usually needed by the companies and organizations that produce them, and they help those companies and organizations do what they need to do. Quite simply, it's the reason that there are so many newsletters and the reason people keep doing them.

Newsletters fulfill another valuable function. They provide good practice for writers just getting started. In fact, it would be surprising if many of you reading this book don't already have a newsletter or two under your belt. There are some good books on doing newsletters – and, as noted, some great templates so that your writing will look good (one reason many dislike newsletters is they often look ghastly).

If you're working on a newsletter, get one of those books and look at some of those templates. Meanwhile, here are a few:

1. **Get a clear idea of the marketing reason for your newsletter.** Fundraising, reinforcing relationships, sharing news of the organization, or selling in some sort of new product or service. Sometimes it's as simple as helping dues-paying members feel that they're getting something and that the organization is doing something. Or it's about creating good will.

2. **Try to offer value to the reader.** Sometimes I feel I have seen and read all the "tips" I can take, but, then again, you're reading some tips right now. So, if it's appropriate, be helpful.

3. **Be interesting.** Photos. Captions. News. Humor. Just because it's a humble little newsletter doesn't mean it can't be good reading. Years ago, an advertising copywriter who loved fishing in West Yellowstone Montana decided that he would support his fishing habit with a newsletter that shared all the news fit to print from West Yellowstone and

107

his fertile imagination. And the *Wretched Mess News* was born – passed from hand to hand and subscribed to by those who wanted a monthly chuckle.

4. **Look good.** Remember that most of us skim. We don't read everything from page one to the end. We look at headlines and photos and, when we see what interests us, we focus in and read further. So don't get all wrapped up in long pieces that go page after page. With the good-looking templates available, you can look like you had an award-winning designer on your editorial staff. And, if there is some article or other fairly lengthy piece (a list of donors, an article that, if shortened, would cause a fuss from the Chairman of the Board), well, that's what all those back pages are for.

5. **Keep it up.** You'd be surprised how often newsletters are read. Certainly not by everybody, but they are read by your loyal customers, your membership, those who want to know more, and maybe someone who is actually interested in your organization or those products and/or services. Make it worth reading – show some humanity – connect with the reader. Project the personality of the brand or the organization. Over the long haul, that little newsletter could be an important piece of the puzzle that adds up to success.

Sure there are a lot of ordinary newsletters that, correctly, get ignored. But the opportunity is there for every writer to do something special. And those trivial little newsletters can be a useful first step in building a successful writing career. And that's not trivial at all.

A Writing Exercise

1. Choose your subject and create a four-page newsletter. (While the designer or art director is probably the best person to address layout and visual issues, content is the writer's domain. Just focus on the writing.) If you can, find a format or template you like and use that as the graphic underpinning.

2. Write eight to ten headings for categories of information to be covered in the newsletter – features developed or submitted by readers. The headings might include: top story, late news, overheard, dates to remember, personality, doing something, a Top Ten list, away from the job, something you didn't know, tips for saving, tips for better health, tips for conserving energy, your turn...

3. Write at least one paragraph to go with each heading.

4. Though most newsletters adopt the format of "mini-newspapers" their content is more feature oriented, allowing the writer to bend the rules to be more friendly, conversational, less grammatical, and more opinionated. Use teasers, factoids, quotations, humor, art, and anecdotes freely.

5. Remember that the purpose of a newsletter is to create a connection between its publisher and its reader, as well as to provide information.

Good writers are those who keep the language efficient.
— **Ezra Pound**

Writing for Today's Brutally Tough Market...

...was how the literary agent described the marketplace in the summer of 2001. Few would disagree with his assessment. I seemed to remember hearing the book market described in very similar words a decade earlier and a decade before that. And the writer of articles for magazine or newspaper publication is used to not having calls returned or letters answered.

"Write a query letter; ask editors or publishers if they are interested before sending a manuscript to them," the writing guides all say. The idea seems to make sense to everyone except editors and publishers who receive hundreds of such letters each month and send computer generated replies of "no thanks," if they reply at all. For an eager author seeking a publishing deal, was the market ever anything other than brutally tough? Most writers have files full of rejection notices from publishers who never saw – much less read – the work they rejected.

Michael Korda tells the story of his great pleasure as a young editor receiving a manuscript he strongly recommended for publication, only to have his bosses at Simon and Schuster take a pass on an unknown author's first novel. And so it was that a more modest publishing house in Boston, Little Brown & Company, was left to publish J.D. Salinger's *The Catcher in the Rye*, a book that consistently outsells thousands of other titles more than 50 years after its first editions reached bookstores.

It's a tale to make a sad writer smile and there are thousands more like it, with only the names changed. *Chicken Soup for the Soul* was rejected by 34 publishers before a small company called

Health Communications accepted it, sold millions of copies, and spun off a series of *Chicken Soup* books that became virtually a category in itself.

John Kennedy Toole's mother, 11 years after her son had taken his life, did what he had been unable to do; she found a publisher for his novel, *A Confederacy of Dunces* in 1980. It won a Pulitzer Prize a year later and has never been out of print since.

Most writers have their first work turned down. Once published, many go on to then have their second books rejected. It is a misconception that once a writer becomes a "published author" he or she has broken through a barrier and becomes an insider – a member of the club – who never again has to stand in line in hopes of being let in. But for a handful of notable exceptions, published authors' proposals – even those of best-selling authors – continue to be subjected to the same review process as first-time authors. Steven King is not included in that group. Martin Amis is.

Sixteen large New York publishers rejected James Brady's novel of the Korean War, *The Marines of Autumn*, in 1992 and '93. Seven years later, it was finally sold to a publisher and ten days before publication, it had gone into its third printing. It was Brady's 13th book.

Of an unknown number of books written each year, a few thousand are published and a few hundred sell really well. Less than a dozen will be remembered a year or two later. Like the performer who dreams of just getting up there on stage once or the athlete who only needs to play one game to make the fantasy a reality, many writers just want to see their names on a book. It's okay if no one buys the book. They did it – start to finish and it has a front cover, a back cover, and a spine. Maybe it even has an author photo on it somewhere.

In 1998 Pushcart Press published a book titled *Pushcart's Complete Rotten Reviews & Rejections*, edited by Bill Henderson and Andre Bernard. As the title suggests, it is a collection of pans and dismissals for the works of writers from W.H. Auden and Jane Austen to Walt Whitman, Oscar Wilde, and Virginia Woolf. Suffice it to say, they did not abandon their aspirations to write and you may have heard of them.

Writers write. The book or the finished article or story is a validation, but most writers will say they did not choose writing as much as writing chose them. It was something they simply had to do. Whatever else they do, many writers cannot imagine not writing. Perhaps it's a journal or poetry or, as Hugh Prather once titled his slim volume of verses, *Notes to Myself*. The joy of seeing the work in a bound, published book or in a magazine is real. But there is a satisfaction that starts long before that important moment. It is the feeling that comes from the writing itself. And the brutally tough market means nothing to it.

Those who tell you it's tough at the top have never been at the bottom.
— **Joe Harvey**

There's a hell of a distance between wisecracking and wit. Wit has truth to it; wisecracking is simply calisthenics with words.
— **Dorothy Parker**

You must keep sending work out; you must never let a manuscript do nothing but eat its head off in a drawer. You send that work out again and again, while you're working on another one. If you have talent, you will receive some measure of success - but only if you persist.
— **Isaac Asimov**

A Writing Exercise

1. Begin listing your own goals for your writing. Perhaps your plan is to "write for yourself" and not pursue publication, which is certainly a personal option...

2. If you do choose to pursue publication of your writing, focus on the types of writing you aspire to do – newspaper writing, novels, poetry, screenplays, etc.

3. Write a "treatment" – an outline or synopsis of the piece you want to write.

4. Check the major directories, *Writers Market* and *Literary Market Place* to note what companies publish the kind of writing you want to do.

5. Check the catalogs of the identified companies online to see how many titles they have in print of the type of work you want to create.

6. Note if you need an agent to help you present your work to them.

7. Start writing.

Writing for Self-Publication...

...was long regarded by professional writers, editors, and most members of the public who were aware of the practice, as writing for self-gratification, a vanity exercise. It was even commonly referred to as "vanity publishing." Quality was irrelevant. The fact that it was self-published carried one overriding message that was assumed: the author could not find a "real" book publisher willing to publish the work. But that's changed, in part because the Internet has allowed and encouraged self-publishing through blogs and posting. And also because desk-top publishing and related technology has made short-run printing production much more affordable – with first-class results. In the twenty-first century the marketplace has shifted dramatically from vanity to being about having something to say, as much as something to sell.

Writers who want to present their messages in their own terms, minus the often-heavy hand of an editor or publisher can do it. Consultants who want to promote their expertise and companies that have a good reason to memorialize their history find that writing and publishing a book can make a lot of business sense.

The Internet and technology have redefined communicating, selling, informing, influencing, and educating. Bloggers, the authors of blogs – the shorthand version of Web log – were first accorded credibility in 2004 as the modern embodiment of the power of the press, rivaling television, newspapers, and mail as a means of reaching a mass audience. Today many of the best-known professional writers have joined the ranks of first-time authors and "citizen journalists."

Self-publishing on the Internet is an inexpensive way of reaching a mass of people. Then again, so is shouting from a rooftop.

In much the same way, some people have something important to say, while others are just shouting. The roads, however, can't be blamed for bad drivers. And, as our tastes and styles evolve, technology, the Internet, or World Wide Web can help new talent find their way at the same time that we will certainly see entirely too much trash online as well.

Then again, D.H. Lawrence, Henry Miller, and Oscar Wilde were called obscene by many religious and political leaders, while others saw them as artists and poets. Times change. Tastes change.

Now let's talk about you. If you've written something that you think is worth reading, you no longer have to let some little thing like not having a publisher stand in your way. Self-published work, vanity publishing, or mainstream commercial media are all equally acceptable today. In fact, Amazon is even there to help you with a "POD" (Publish on Demand) service. Yet the fact remains that writing still needs to be worth a reader's time. So even though new opportunities in publishing offer new opportunities for entrepreneurial writers and even though it no longer matters as much who or what is listed as publisher, the fact remains... it's still about the words.

Perhaps it would be better not to be a writer, but if you must, then write. If all feels hopeless, if that famous 'inspiration' will not come, write. If you are a genius, you'll make your own rules, but if not – and the odds are against it – go to your desk no matter what your mood, face the icy challenge of the paper – write.
— **J. B. Priestly**

Great spirits have always encountered violent opposition from mediocre minds.
— **Albert Einstein**

The Writing Life...

...holds the promise of wealth, fame, romance, passion, and world-wide acclaim, as well as a warning for aspiring writers to not give up your day job.

Most authors are hyphenated, as in "author-anthropologist" or "author-tap dancer" or "author-coal miner." That is to say, with sweeping generalization, that a vast majority of writers who are only writers are broke most of the time.

In 2003 the average book advance was $5,000. That was the average – meaning former President Clinton received an $8 million advance to write his book and somebody named Larry in Daytona Beach, Florida got a dollar to make the publishing contract legal. Most writers' advances against royalties fall some-where in between, though more were on Larry's side of the line than were with President Clinton, with all due respect.

Writing can be a very emotional business, both as a process and as a career. Someone who walks away from a job as a computer programmer, a construction worker, or vice president of practically anything is not likely to experience the same sense of deflation as that felt by the writer, who is usually not giving up a job as much as he or she is giving up a long-held dream.

It is a challenge each month for most writers to pay their bills. Even many of the best known authors, men and women who could not imagine doing anything else and have been recognized with various honors, owe money to everyone they know. And as for the not-so-famous writers, they are like the guy with the broom, walking behind the circus elephant, just happy to be in show business.

So what makes writers pile up boxes of rejection letters and keep going? Can it be all just hope and dreams and ego?

A guy told everyone he wrote for the *New Yorker*, although the *New Yorker* was not aware of that. No matter. As far as he was concerned, he was writing for the *New Yorker* and one day, he was sure, his writing would appear there.

People who call themselves writers, but spend more time imagining what they will wear for their book jacket photo or thinking about their interview on the *Today Show*, aren't so much aspiring writers as they are aspiring celebrities. Writers write quarterly reports for mutual funds, brochures for car dealers, and descriptions of umbrellas for general merchandise catalogs. If someday they sell a screenplay or a novel or a memoir… that would be good too. Meanwhile, they are writers and that's what they want to do.

The image of the writer who sleeps all day and writes all night or spends the day in a bathrobe or takes long walks or discussing trade deficits with his or her dog is totally accurate. So is the one of the writer who outlines, writes and rewrites, painstakingly massaging sentences and paragraphs to a fine polish and the writer who completes three or four books in a year. During Isaac Asimov's most productive period, he reportedly produced 13 books in one year. Other writers take several years to complete one book. According to comments from editors, most writers are living contradictions. And neurotics.

Often intense, anxious, unpredictable, unreliable, loyal, disciplined, imaginative, and funny, fiction writers create themselves in the images of people they admire or want to be. And like characters in their stories, they go on to reinvent themselves again and again. Writing nonfiction, whether serious financial bulletins, scholarly papers, or gags, is no less agonizing than fiction as it takes shape and evolves into a fully completed work, presenting the writer's talent, as well as the subject to be shared, examined, and considered.

Writers of books are thought to be among the lucky ones. They know the feeling that comes from creating something that will be appreciated by some, derided by others, but will nonetheless represent an achievement that a relative few can claim, even if the book is never published. Because for all the people who insist they could write a book, it was the writer who actually did.

I write for the same reason I breathe - because if I didn't, I would die.
— **Isaac Asimov**

Write quickly and you will never write well.
Write well, and you will soon write quickly.
— **Marcus Fabius Quintilianus, 65 A.D.**

A writer needs three things, experience, observation, and imagination, any two of which, at times any one of which,
can supply the lack of the others.
— **William Faulkner**

Writing Rhetoric…

…requires first understanding what rhetoric is. By definition, rhetoric is the art of using language effectively and persuasively. It's communicating a particular idea in a particular situation. But how then is writing rhetoric different from what any other type of good writing should be?

In a broad sense, it's not. In a more finite application, rhetoric is also a style of speaking or writing, especially the language of a particular subject, as in "fiery political rhetoric." It can also be using language that is elaborate, pretentious, insincere, or intellectually vacuous.

Whoa. Pretentious? Insincere? Intellectually vacuous? Strong stuff.

Why would colleges and universities offer entire courses that propose to teach people to write rhetoric if rhetoric is, by some definitions, pretentious, insincere, and/or intellectually vacuous? The fact is that rhetoric is a term used in a variety of forms and can mean many things.

In the first decade of the twenty-first century, politicians were held in particularly low esteem by much of the general public – a status, in fact, not unique to that time in history. Perhaps the "pretentious, insincere, and intellectually vacuous" designation was intended to be applied more toward political rhetoric, one of the most common forms. Politicians begin with a hard premise, then write and speak emphatically to that premise, positing that it represents an indisputable truth, even if facts or interpretation support a contradictory view.

There are five essential elements of rhetoric: the communicator – who is delivering the message; the audience – taking into account the predispositions or lack of them among readers or listeners; the subject, the objective, and the language or medium. Applying these elements, through one or a variety of approaches, is how written words accomplish a writer's specific objectives with an intended audience.

Ethos, Pathos, and Logos.

Writers, like politicians, use rhetoric to make a persuasive case and this is the sense in which rhetoric is considered an art. That is, persuasion is not simply "making a case," but applying specific techniques for making a case. Here, rhetoric may take one or more of three distinct approaches: pathos, a persuasive approach that appeals to emotions; ethos, which tries to make a persuasive case based on the credibility of the argument; and logos, a persuasive technique that relies on logic to make its case.

What is important to know – and where so many politicians miss their mark – is that a single persuasive approach or technique will not likely be effective with all subjects and all audiences. People have differing ideas about what is credible or logical and certainly not everyone responds to subjects on the same emotional level. It is for this reason that writers for politicians attempt to employ rhetoric of a broader, more general type, such as citing the importance of helping children or those in need or doing what is right and just, without getting specific as to exactly who or what those terms cover.

Non-politicians – writers making a case on a specific point, on behalf of a cause or issue – can use rhetoric more freely and with intense passion to appeal to readers' emotions, as well as pressing points using logic and framing credible arguments that are sure to pass "the smell test" – one of the more descriptive expressions to define the believability of a particular argument.

Rhetoric as a form of writing is distinct from journalism in that, while both insist the writer present facts – who, what, when, where, why, and how – journalism, at its best, is unbiased, whereas rhetoric is the opposite; taking a position and persuasively, ideally eloquently, making a case for its acceptance.

Aristotle wrote extensively on the power of rhetoric and St. Augustine, as both a writer and teacher of rhetoric, recognized its importance in effective communication in the pursuit of truth, as well as the spread of Christianity.

Such understanding is no less valuable for writers attempting to communicate effectively today.

My task... is, by the power of the written word to make you hear, to make you feel – it is, before all, to make you see. That – and no more – and it is everything.
— **Joseph Conrad**

If you would write emotionally, be first unemotional. If you would move your readers to tears, do not let them see you cry.
— **James J. Kilpatrick**

Sometimes I think it is a great mistake to have matter that can think and feel. It complains so. By the same token, though, I suppose that boulders and mountains and moons could be accused of being a little too phlegmatic.
— **Kurt Vonnegut**

A Writing Exercise

1. Select a subject about which you feel very strongly, such as religion, politics, the environment, media bias, race relations, cultural heritage, or another topic.

2. Write side-by-side lists of opposing points of view on that subject.

3. Imagine a debate in which to people present these opposing points of view.

4. With yourself in the role of speechwriter, write a one-minute opening statement – about 300 words – for the debater whose position most closely parallels your own.

5. Use the elements of rhetoric as described in this chapter essay.

A Writer's Pen...

If writing is only about talent, why do people seem to care so much how writers write? Maybe it's because writing is only mostly about talent – and skill and appreciation of language – what some might describe as "having a way with words."

Writers have their various individual ways of getting words on paper. For some, it's a matter of attitude, waking up early and going for walks or meditating or performing a type of ritual before the words will flow. Others need the quiet of night, background music, or a window with a view for inspiration, or absolute privacy and no window or music. Pretty much everyone needs his or her "tools" which can include such things as coffee (or something stronger), cigarettes, candy bars, or a cat. For the author of this work, it's a pen.

I love pens. More specifically, the ones pen makers call "fine writing instruments." I wrote my first book with a black fountain pen that was ultra-slim and made of metal. I used that pen for a lot of writing, but when I uncapped it to work on my book, it was as if it straightened up, cleared its throat and said, okay, get serious now; this one's going in the public library.

When I signed the contract for my second book, I marked the occasion by buying a new pen that cost several hundred dollars – a ridiculous amount and certainly the most I'd ever paid for a pen. I used it to write a book that was fairly successful and that success created a sort of bond between the pen and me. Years later, I gave that pen to the son of a man I had admired for much of my life. The young man had written a book about his late father. When my wife and I noticed he was signing copies of the book with a pen like the ones hotels leave next to telephones and ashtrays, we exchanged sad expressions. I offered him my pen and he noticed the difference the first time he signed his name with it. We told him to keep it – that he needed a writer's pen.

Later, my wife felt sad since she knew that particular pen had a special significance to me. I told her it was all right – that it still did, only now the significance was different. It was in the hand of a great man's son, who was using it to sign his name in books that would keep his father's memory alive.

The next day, my wife gave me a pen identical to the one I had given away. This one now had a significance of its own.

Then the editor of my first two books gave me an elegant fountain pen that was made the year I was born.

Images come to mind when I see paintings of Shakespeare and Charles Dickens with their quill pens in hands, or the wonderful painting by Vanessa Bell of Leonard Woolf that was used on the jacket of David Lodge's excellent book, *The Practice of Writing*. I can see the pen he's holding in the painting moving across the page and I imagine the members of the Bloomsbury Group nearby, just out of the frame, creating words, pictures, and ideas that would be talked about for generations.

Over the years, I've accumulated several more really good pens, many of them thoughtfully chosen as gifts for me from my wife or from friends. One was from my daughter. Another, I bought on a trip to France. Still another belonged to a relative from an earlier generation.

Ten books later, I sat at my desk with four wooden boxes of fine pens in front of me and a few more tucked away in briefcases and pockets. I write on lined white pads of paper or in a journal or on note cards. The actual act of writing is as much a part of the process for me as the finished pages, how the words get from me onto the paper.

I know writers who are crazy about their word-processors or notebook computers with all their grand programs and hi-tech features. They can't understand why someone would want to write any other way. But, to me, writing is not about "processing words" or "computing." It's about writing.

Obviously, in the twenty-first century, sales of quill pens are at perhaps an all-time low, and most editors, publishers, instructors, and businesses use and insist on word processors and computers to generate written material. But good writing starts with the writer and every writer should find the method that helps produce his or her best work.

So when people ask me how to get started writing, I tell them I think having something to say is important; then think about who will read what you write and how it can be presented in a way that is different from what's come before, as well as being interesting, informative, or entertaining.

Then I tell them to get a good pen.

The pen is mightier than the sword.
— **William Shakespeare**

The pen became a clarion.
— **Henry Wadsworth Longfellow**

The feather, whence the pen
Was shaped that traced the lives of these good men,
Dropped from an Angel's wing.
— **William Wordsworth,**

With a single Wirt pen I have earned the family's living for
many years. With two, I could have grown rich.
— **Mark Twain,**
in a letter to the Wirt Fountain Pen Company, in 1898

A Writing Exercise

Writers should not be bound by doing something a certain way because that's how it has always been done or the way they routinely do it.

A final presentation of material may have to be in a format that, for any number of reasons, is standard or acceptable to the recipient, but the process by which it gets to that place should allow the writer to operate at his or her best.

Experiment, trying different writing instruments and environments to learn when, where, and how you produce your best work. For some people the differences are slight or not noticeable, but others find the place, time of day, and tools involved can make a big difference in the quality of their writing or in "finding the writer's voice."

1. Create a paragraph and write it using a variety of writing instruments – word processor, pencil, typewriter, ballpoint pen, roller ball, fountain pen, or even a quill pen, if you can find one.

2. Note the differences in how it feels to write with each different instrument, in terms of not only comfort, but of the total experience.

3. Note that most written material today must be submitted in typewritten form using a word processor or a computer, but notes and early drafts should be written in the form that is most comfortable and allows the writer to write his or her best.

Writing Propaganda...

...is a generally misunderstood proposition. That is because the term "propaganda" does not actually mean what most people think it means. Propaganda is defined as the activity of spreading particular ideas or opinions according to an organized plan. That seems harmless enough. The American Heritage Dictionary goes a bit further, declaring it is official government communications to the public that are designed to influence opinion. The information may be true or false, but it is always carefully selected for its political effect. The second definition is the one that tends to unsettle people – particularly the part that says the information can be false. One year, the legendary San Francisco ad man Howard Gossage taught a course at Penn State. The title of his course: "The Nature of Paid Propaganda." Before he delivered a single word in class, he managed to create quite a bit of controversy, which, of course, was Howard's objective.

"When most people think about propaganda, they think of the enormous 'Big Lie' campaigns waged by Hitler and Stalin in the 1930s," explains Trinity University professor Dr. Aaron Delwiche. "Since nothing comparable is being disseminated in our society today, many believe that propaganda is no longer an issue."

Dr. Delwiche was perhaps speaking generally of modern times in his reference to today. But, in fact, some would insist that the political climate of the first decade of the twenty-first century was heavy with propaganda campaigns initiated by the government, various religious leaders, environmental experts, special interest groups of every stripe, and, of course, politicians.

"Propaganda can be as blatant as a swastika or as subtle as a joke," notes Dr. Delwiche. "Its persuasive techniques are regularly applied by politicians, advertisers, journalists, radio personalities, and others who are interested in influencing human behavior. Propagandistic messages can be used to accomplish positive social ends, as in campaigns to reduce drunk driving, but they are also used to win elections and to sell malt liquor."

Herein lies the confusion. World War II propagandists spread disinformation that was termed propaganda, so the word became synonymous with campaigns of disinformation. How then does one accept the same term being applied to something positive, such as a campaign to reduce reckless or drunk driving?

The operative word is "accept," and it is how public relations defines the process. For all the lofty definitions the trade associations confer on it, public relations is the art or science of influencing or persuading. From written press releases and printed collateral materials to speaking tours, carefully placed articles, interviews, and personal appearances, the subject is the "product" positioned, promoted, merchandised, and marketed in a calculated campaign to generate acceptance and secure a commitment of support.

A well-managed public relations effort and a propaganda campaign are essentially the same, except that propaganda has, like spin, grown to have an unsavory connotation as people holding contrary or opposing views have described as propaganda anything they hope the public will treat in a dismissive or suspect manner.

Given that reality, practitioners would be wise to follow Julia Child's advice about serving something that didn't turn out right, when presenting a campaign that is essentially propaganda… call it something else. But whatever we call it, as citizens we should learn to recognize it – and, as writing professionals – when we have the task of persuading people before us, we should know how to do it.

A Writing Exercise

1. Find an example of propaganda in a daily newspaper – an idea or subject of an article that is clearly intended to influence, rather than to simply inform, the reader.

2. Rewrite the article in such a way that it is a straight news story, not a propaganda initiative.

At its root, propaganda plays on emotions, often defying reason and facts in order to reach into the psyche of the audience. Propaganda is a mind game – the skillful propagandist plays with your deepest emotions, exploiting your greatest fears and prejudices.
— **from an Op Ed piece in the** *Seattle Times*

If those in charge of our society - politicians, corporate executives, and owners of press and television - can dominate our ideas, they will be secure in their power. They will not need soldiers patrolling the streets. We will control ourselves.
— **Howard Zinn**

A propagandist is a specialist in selling attitudes and opinions.
— **Hans Speier**

We trust Americans to recognize propaganda and misinformation, and to make their own decisions about what they read and believe.
— **The American Library Association**

Writing a Marketing Plan...

...is a particularly important skill for business writers, particularly since marketing is a critical aspect of virtually every company or organization. The process and format for writing marketing plans is similar to that for writing plans for PR and advertising campaigns. PR and advertising plans are, essentially, subsets of the marketing plan. It is also important to understand that the marketing plan is not the same as the business plan. The marketing plan is a subset of the business plan, which should include at least a basic marketing plan as a component.

A business plan is what a business owner presents to investors or a bank when looking for a loan or for investment capital. It identifies essentially what the business is set up to do, how it will do it, and what it will take in terms of people, facilities, equipment, materials, and funding to reach stated business and financial objectives.

Marketing is the umbrella term for a variety of disciplines that help you bring a business or service to the marketplace. It can include packaging, positioning, pricing, promotion, distribution, and sales. Advertising and public relations are important parts of the marketing mix for virtually every business. Within the marketing plan, they are usually identified for budget purposes under promotion.

Assuming the product or service is of acceptable quality, marketing is often the pivotal element in achieving success.

The marketing plan is the checklist, outline, and roadmap for the marketing program and someone has to start it somewhere by writing it. While developing the content and doing the background work is a challenge, the actual writing of the marketing plan is not always an especially creative undertaking. It has more to do with being clear, accurate, and holding to the generally accepted format for these documents.

While it rarely falls to the writer to make the decisions about what goes into the marketing plan, the writer must know the elements of the marketing plan format and what questions to ask to acquire the information needed to create a viable plan. The writer must ask the marketer for the following.

- Situation analysis (what the situation is that the plan needs to address). There are some fairly standard elements within that situation analysis. It will cover the size of the market, the current competitive situation, who uses the product or service, and other aspects such as purchase cycle and seasonality (how often and when the product or service is used). Some additional research may be recommended.

- Statement of objectives (what the plan is supposed to accomplish).

- Strategy for achieving the objectives.

- Tactics to be employed to execute the strategy.

- Budget, specifying the amount available to implement the tactics.

- Timeline, noting how long a time has been allowed for executing the plan within the allotted budget to achieve the objective.

With the marketer supplying the answers and the necessary information, the writer then needs to assemble the information, with appropriate subheads and footnotes.

Some marketing plans are months or more in development. The result is a voluminous document that is designed to impress boards of directors, but that, in my experience, never get read – much less used.

The best marketing plans should be no longer than they need

to be for easy distribution and execution. A few pages seems to be a normal length, but I've also seen them fill a binder of some thickness. If you get good at writing these sorts of documents, which also grow into other related types – business proposals, marketing plans for new products, and, of course, the PR and advertising plans that go along with a company's marketing – you may have a lot of interesting work ahead of you.

In general, marketing plans are much less satisfying to a writer than creating a novel or a screenplay, but they're a lot more interesting than some other types of writing. The marketing plan is of paramount importance to a business or organization. Writers who perform this task with distinction can find it rewarding in terms of both financial remuneration and the contribution to building a uniquely effective and successful company.

A Writing Exercise

1. Choose a company, organization, or product as your subject – perhaps a noteworthy cause, a candidate for public office, a personal computer, cell phone, a favorite brand of toothpaste, a candy bar, or a restaurant.

2. Write a marketing plan for your subject company or brand, noting its situation analysis (what the situation is that the plan needs to address); objectives (what the plan is supposed to accomplish); strategy for achieving the objectives; tactics; budget; and timeline.

3. Make it concise and specific as to what it will accomplish.

Writing for Newspapers...

...was the stuff dreams were made on. Generations of young people aspired to be newspaper writers, inspired by the work of intrepid legendary reporters and columnists, from Nellie Bly, A.J. Liebling, Ernie Pyle, and Edward R. Murrow to Mike Royko, Jimmy Breslin, and Woodward and Bernstein. These were only a few giants of the press who rose to define and distinguish the profession, reporting the news, breaking important stories, going on to write books, and, in some cases, having books written about them.

The newspaper reporter – the journalist – was, for many, just an average, honest person with a bigger than average job.

From the beginning to the present, there have always been journalists who misused or abused the public trust to fulfill their own ambitions or agenda. On the other side, however, are those who attack and attempt to diminish journalists when it serves their purposes. The value of the press in a free society has always been accepted, though it becomes a frequent target of attacks by factions attempting to downplay the importance of the media when it produces information that is at odds with the objectives of these groups.

It is true that the standing of media among much of the public declined during the decades since the 1970s, but much of the purported distrust may well be manufactured. Some of the news media's fall from favor has been deserved, though much of it has been the result of powerful interests undermining the press to minimize the impact of corporate and political misconduct the press exposed.

Respected and influential figures in both TV journalism and

the literary profession began their careers as newspaper reporters. The novelist Kurt Vonnegut once worked as a reporter for *City News Bureau* in Chicago. David Halberstam and Gay Talese were both reporters for the *New York Times*; and even the late President John F. Kennedy had a brief career as a newspaper reporter before entering Congress. It's long been regarded as a truly noble profession.

Originally the term "the press" referred only to newspapers, but today, with the proliferation of new media formats, it encompasses many and broader entities, most particularly the "citizen journalists" who make their mark as bloggers. But newspaper writers are still regarded as the elite of the profession and are perhaps the most serious and respected among media chroniclers.

The press is often referred to as the Fourth Estate, a term that can be traced back to historian Thomas Carlysle in the early 19th century. Reportedly in May of 1789, Louis XVI summoned to Versailles a full meeting of the Estate General, an assembly of representatives from all but the poorest segment of French citizenry. The First Estate consisted of 300 members of the clergy; the Second Estate was 300 nobles; and the Third Estate included 600 commoners. Years later, following the French Revolution, the British statesman Edmund Burke, looking up at the Press Gallery of the House of Commons, said, "Yonder sits the Fourth Estate, and they are more important than them all."

The newspaper profession – journalism – is not just a job or a career, it is a responsibility held sacred by the Founding Fathers of the United States.

Thomas Jefferson, said famously on the necessity of a free press, "The basis of our government being the opinion of the people, the very first object should be to keep that right; and were it left to me to decide whether we should have a government without newspapers, or newspapers without a government, I should not hesitate a moment to prefer the latter."

The newspaper business attracts a certain type of individual, usually curious and idealistic – someone who needs or chooses to be part of the process of finding better solutions to problems and making a difference. A newspaper is still considered the best "training ground" for reporters of any media – the place to learn the business and the rules, working with knowledgeable editors and seasoned professionals. The reporter's job is to gather and analyze facts about events through observation and investigation, and write stories describing those events, their meaning, and effects.

A reporter could be on "general assignment," meaning following up on whatever the editor directs him or her to do; on "special assignment," which involves in-depth work on a particular story; or a regular "beat" providing ongoing reports on a particular industry or segment of society, reporting on crime, politics, sports, business, entertainment, local news, or other areas. A feature reporter covers news in specialized areas, such as medicine, foreign affairs, consumer affairs, education, or labor.

Through the centuries, writers for newspapers have been guided by basic rules of journalism, reporting who, what, when, where, why, and how, and adhering to high standards and a code of professional conduct, of fairness and integrity. Ethics have always been central to the process and the profession. The quality of the writing may vary from writer to writer, but preserving the distinguished history and legacy of the press is second in importance to few others. Among writers, newspaper writers and reporters – journalists – continue to be, if not a cut above, certainly first among equals.

A Writing Exercise

1. Choose a national news story with an Associated Press (AP) byline or source from a newspaper or online.

2. Find a story on that same subject (same date) written by a newspaper staff writer or independent journalist, not associated with the wire service (AP).

3. Note and compare any differences in content and style between the two stories.

Writing for the Media...

...is a phrase that might seem awkward or redundant. With the exception of writing letters home or writing daily in a journal or preparing a business proposal or a shopping list, most writing is for media, whether it's for a newspaper or TV, magazines, radio, the Internet, or advertising copy or press releases.

What writers need to understand about writing for media is the distinctions and differences – what part of the media is a writer writing for.

Good writing skills and the ability to communicate *who*, *what*, *when*, *where*, *why*, and *how* succinctly and effectively are essential. But an appreciation of where the mindset of the reader lies and why certain types of people seek, value, and attach credibility and legitimacy to some media and not others is the reality of communication today.

Readers have "mental filters" that process what they read through their own belief systems, sometimes attaching a particular tone, slant or something that isn't there to a piece of writing.

But writers – and certainly much of the public – need to be reminded often that media is a plural term and a writer can't write the same for TV or radio as for print and can't write the same way for the *Wall Street Journal* as he or she might for *People* or *Rolling Stone*.

Readers and viewers understand the differences between entertainment media, sports media, public affairs media, special interest media, and general interest media. Even within these and other categories, media entities are not alike, nor frequently even similar.

Properties within a particular branch of media, newspapers, for example, can be highly unique, regionally, economically, ethnically, demographically, or ideologically distinctive in their presentation of content. That is one reason why when critics accuse "the media" of showing a bias or of having a particular point of view, the charge is virtually impossible to support and is basically reflecting the simplistic opinion of the accuser. Writers need to know this and have an appreciation of how it may or may not influence particular media content.

The "mainstream media" is a term that has grown in usage. Critics and those having an adversarial relationship with some segments of the media created the term. These individuals charge media bias when media reflects a consensus of opinion that works against their interests.

The designation of "the mainstream media" is meant to include major U.S. television networks (ABC, CBS, and NBC, as well as PBS and cable TV channels CNN and MSNBC), and the *New York Times*, the *Washington Post*, the *Boston Globe, Los Angeles Times, Chicago Tribune*, and the *San Francisco Chronicle, Time* magazine and *Newsweek*.

These properties are also largely characterized as the "media establishment" and described as either very or somewhat "liberal" or "moderate" or "progressive" in their reporting and socio-political slant, despite having relatively conservative corporate owners.

TV's Fox News Channel is the highest rated cable news channel in the first decade of the 21st century; the *Wall Street Journal* and Gannett's *USA Today* are two of the few national daily newspapers that are financially successful and reach millions of readers each day. The *New York Post* and *Houston Chronicle* are not considered part of the "mainstream media" despite their being among the nation's most frequently read daily newspapers. The reasoning on this is that they are not considered to be "liberal" media, and "mainstream" is the label conservatives applied to media that does not share its views.

Coining the term "mainstream media" is an attempt to segregate, lump together, and systematically diminish and discredit media that does not inherently support its critics' ideological position.

Among weekly special interest magazines, readers with a moderate or liberal point of view appreciate news coverage and commentary that appears in the *Nation* and the *New Republic*. Their conservative counterparts read the *National Review* and the *Weekly Standard*. Neither group attaches much credibility to the content of the other group's reading choices and they have been known to argue about who has claim or closer ties to people who read *Sports Illustrated*, as if every member of the public is aligned with a political ideology or has singular tastes.

Writers need to be plugged in to this notion in order to deliver what editors and their constituents expect of them. In terms of style, tone, and perspective, different readers, even within a particular city (when choices are available), will be drawn to the newspaper, channel, or programming that reflects not only their tastes, but their ideology.

The list of the top newspapers in the U.S. (by circulation) shows that, from New York to San Francisco and St. Petersburg to Boston, people are reading the news as presented to them by the media, but many hold that it is not the same news being reported in terms of the "slant" – the bias or emphasis on certain points and comments – of the news-gathering and reporting entity.

To millions of newspaper readers across the United States and around the world, what is reported or written becomes secondary to a perception of how it is reported or written. Regardless of quality of a written piece, the subjectivity of the reader – the inner voice that is taking in the information read and processing it – is making a judgment on the perceived fairness or bias of the writer. It makes writing for the media even more challenging, as readers form opinions on the merit of writing based on not so much what they read, but what they think they read.

The newspapers on this list provide information to people across the United States. Some of the newspapers are regarded as good, some less than good. Some are considered liberal, some conservative, and as such reflecting their owners' or editorial staff bias. Few publishers will publicly concede the opinions of them held by their critics are fair. Writers for these publications and their broadcast and cable counterparts must be mindful of both their own standards of fairness and the perceptions of their publics.

Here, from the Audit Bureau of Circulations, are the top 25 daily newspapers in the U.S. by circulation for the six-month period ending March 31, 2008:

1. *USA Today*: 2,284,219
2. The *Wall Street Journal*: 2,069,463
3. The *New York Times*: 1,077,256
4. *Los Angeles Times*: 773,884
5. The *Daily News* - New York, NY: 703,137
6. The *New York Post*: 702,488
7. *Washington Post*: 673,180
8. *Chicago Tribune*: 541,663
9. *Houston Chronicle*: 494,131
10. *Arizona Republic* - Phoenix, AZ: 413,332
11. *Newsday* - Melville, NY: 379,613
12. *San Francisco Chronicle*: 370,345
13. *Dallas Morning News*: 368,313
14. The *Boston Globe*: 350,605
15. The *Star-Ledger* - Newark, NJ: 345,130
16. *Philadelphia Inquirer*: 334,150
17. The *Plain Dealer* - Cleveland, OH: 330,280
18. The *Atlanta Journal-Constitution*: 326,907

19. *Star-Tribune* - Minneapolis, MN: 322,362
20. *St. Petersburg Times*:   316,007
21. The *Chicago Sun-Times*:   312,274
22. *Detroit Free Press*:   308,944
23. The *Oregonian* - Portland, OR: 304,399
24. The *San Diego Union Tribune*:   288,669
25. The *Sacramento Bee*:   268,755

You can write about anything, and if you write well enough, even the reader with no intrinsic interest in the subject will become involved.
— **Tracy Kidder**

A Writing Exercise

1. Read an issue of the *Wall Street Journal* and an issue of the *New York Times* from the same day.

2. Select stories on the same subject that appeared in both papers.

3. Underline the points noting who, what, when, and where in both stories.

4. Using a highlighter, mark the adjectives and adverbs in both stories.

5. Write a short essay (250 words) on differences or distinctions in how the two publications treated the story in terms of tone and style.

Writing for Public Relations...

...can be as misunderstood a process as PR itself. It's writing not only with a point of view, but with an objective. PR writing has to accomplish something. It must create awareness, change someone's mind, persuade people to do something, convince an editor, a producer, columnist, or a widely-read blogger to do a story on a particular subject – and, in a perfect world, making them think it was their idea.

Public relations provides a systematic process that utilizes a variety of techniques and disciplines to assure:

(1) that the public or a specific target audience is aware of a subject, and/or

(2) how the public regards the subject both for the near-term and, perhaps, long-term.

PR writing is about presenting information that describes a subject, an issue, or a company in the best possible terms. It demands the crafting of a message or "message points" that convey information, while promoting or advancing a specific point of view.

The most common goal of a public relations effort is to create awareness because market research indicates a better known company, organization, or brand is perceived to be a better company, organization, or brand.

Generating awareness, however, is not – or should not – be the only goal of PR. Although some pundits insist that "any publicity is good publicity" or that they "don't care what is said about them as long as they get the name right," such clichés are not what PR is about. In fact, those two statements get the idea behind PR completely wrong.

Any publicity is not good publicity. A prominent individual charged with a wrongdoing or a business in financial trouble landing on the front page of a newspaper or a magazine cover or an erroneous report circulated across the World Wide Web is not likely to see benefits resulting from such publicity.

Public relations writers are expected to do their homework and understand the workings of the media, as well as legal, cultural, and political considerations related to the subjects about which they write. It is writing more about what the editor, producer, and audience wants and needs than about what the writer wants to write. There is room for expression and creativity in the use of language, but *PR writing must be objective-driven.*

A press release is the basic working tool and product of most PR writers. Its very existence must reflect the benefit of its subject, whether that subject is a product, a person, or a company. PR is both an art and a science, affecting a company's reputation and market position.

PR professionals know that "public" is as much a plural term as "media" and that what's written must appeal to more than one position, attitude or constituent group. The message in the press release – and how it is presented – must reflect sensitivity to a range of situations, from regional bias to gender or ethics or any number of other influences. It's not just putting out a clever, upbeat press release that begins, "It's that time again," and ending up with a story on the cover of *Time* magazine.

Some people regard public relations practitioners as "flacks" or "spin-doctors" – terms used to suggest they are highly skilled and experienced liars. Some probably are. But a talented writer who understands the importance of gauging and influencing public opinion and crafts a message carefully, performs an important information function.

Public relations and advertising are companion disciplines under the marketing umbrella and their respective campaigns usually or frequently have similar objectives. While certain liberties and creative license is permitted in ad copy writing, that's not true of PR writing, the basis of which is principles of journalism. Advertisers choose and control the space in which their messages appear; PR writers must convince others who control space to turn it over to them, along with whatever prestige or stamp of credibility it might carry.

PR writers must continually take the pulse and listen to the voice of the market, then craft messages that will help achieve the desired objective, while reflecting understanding and responding to people's needs and wants.

It is said that *perception is reality*, yet both can all too easily be misidentified or can change without warning.

As with a piece of serious journalism (which some press releases actually are or become, appearing *exactly as written* in the news media), PR stories need to have a point, tell who, what, when, where, why, and how, be informative and persuasive. The PR writer must be a competent writer and must understand also how important it is that the words relate to the public.

Reality is an illusion, albeit a very persistent one.
— **Albert Einstein**

A Writing Exercise

The press release is the primary tool of a public relations practitioner vying for media attention – a story written and placed in a newspaper or magazine, a segment produced for television, a piece presented as a broadcast TV or radio story. This exercise asks the writer to work backwards.

1. Select a story in a newspaper or magazine.

2. Evaluate it for interest and the quality of the writing. Did you learn anything from it?

3. Underline or highlight the basic elements of the story – who, what, when, where, and why.

4. List those elements on a separate sheet.

5. Using the information drawn from the story, write a press release that would have likely led to the story you read.

6. Reread what you wrote and answer the question, If you were an editor receiving this press release, would you use it to develop a story.

Writing Ad Copy...

...is an area where writers are usually not discouraged from ignoring the rules of good writing or grammar. Not that ad copy writers intentionally write badly. They don't. But sentence fragments abound. Exclamation points litter meager lines of text on the premise that people must see excitement indicated on a page, and that no one will read long copy so the phrases (fragments) must be short and punchy. In general, that's a strong premise – or at least it's the conventional wisdom of the advertising industry – but as with most things general, the exceptions get a lot of the attention.

David Ogilvy, the late and legendary founder of the international advertising agency Ogilvy & Mather, wrote long ago, "I don't know the rules of grammar... If you're trying to persuade people to do something, or buy something, it seems to me you should use their language, the language they use every day, the language in which they think."

That makes perfect sense. It also reiterates a basic rule of writing of any kind: Write so people can understand what you're trying to say.

Mr. Ogilvy was not only one of the most respected and influential figures in advertising, he was one of its best and most successful ad copywriters. He loved the advertising business and was one of its biggest boosters, yet, he was not afraid to point out the blemishes among the beauty marks when in situations where he believed his colleagues fell short of the mark.

"Advertising is a business of words," he noted, "but advertising agencies are infested with men and women who cannot write. They cannot write advertisements, and they cannot write plans.

They are helpless as deaf mutes on the stage of the Metropolitan Opera."

A talented man with words, David Ogilvy had little patience for advertising professionals who gave their clients or the public less than good work. He wrote excellent ads that had a lot of copy, but they were so well written that people read them, in defiance of the conventional wisdom. He believed in powerful headlines that got attention, made a promise, and told people what the ad – and the product being advertised – was about. He believed ad copy should be as long as it needed to be.

The common belief is that advertising is about selling something. That's partly true, as advertising is a part of the marketing process, but advertising is not all about selling. Except for direct response ads with 800-numbers or coupons or special offers linked to an immediate call-to-action, ads don't actually sell. Ads are presentations of information intended to create awareness, interest, desire, curiosity, or excitement for a subject, but the typical ad is not a sales rep, check-out counter, or order desk.

Good ads let people know something exists, where to find it, and why they should want to find it.

One very big problem has haunted the advertising industry and adverting itself for decades, the perception that ads lie. The perceptions were proved to be true in so many cases that a "truth in advertising" law was passed to protect the public from false, deceptive, or misleading claims in ads and, alas, in what were too many instances, outright fraud.

Ethics, a subject addressed in virtually all industries, has become a running joke when applied to the advertising business. Much of the public really does think ads lie and advertising people are liars. Ad people rank with politicians and car salesman at the bottom of the public's list in terms of honesty.

Writers usually don't get the last word when it comes to truth in advertising, but they have more than a little to do with the process. Is it not possible to convey a promotional piece of information that gets attention, is interesting, creates a desire for the product, and motivates the public to take action without lying? Of course it is.

Writers create fantasies, helping people imagine what it would be like to soar through space, live underwater, explore jungles, tame frontiers, and bring crowds of people to their feet cheering in a stadium, or be seen and heard by fans around the world through collections of wires and satellite dishes. Writers can make people laugh, make them cry, make them dance, make them applaud and shout by using words and images that are bright and true.

After all that, writers can certainly find the words to make someone want a particular car, coat, or a package of frozen meatballs without lying.

In the words of another advertising legend, Leo Burnett, "Advertising is the ability to sense, interpret… to put the very heart throbs of a business into type, paper and ink."

All the writer has to do is do it.

People read what interests them. Sometimes it's an ad.
— **Howard Luck Gossage**

The first thing one must do to succeed in advertising is to have the attention of the reader. That means to be interesting. The next thing is to stick to the truth, and that means rectifying whatever's wrong in the merchant's business. If the truth isn't tellable, fix it so it is. That is about all there is to it.
— **John E. Powers,**

A Writing Exercise

1. Think of you favorite product – something you own, enjoy, use, or consume virtually every day.

2. Answer these questions:
   a. What does it do?
   b. What's its purpose?
   c. How did you come to use it?
   d. Why do you like it?
   e. What makes it different or better than its competitors or alternatives?
   f. What are the very best things about it?
   g. What made you choose this product?
   h. Would you recommend it to others? If so, why?
   i. Where and how can people find this product?

3. Based on how you answered the above questions, write an ad for the product. Use as many of the points listed as you think you need to make a persuasive case for the product.

Writing Creative Nonfiction...

...might seem like an oxymoron to some people. How can something be creative, a term typically applied to an original work, and be nonfiction, which is by definition reality-based? Can there be such a thing as "original nonfiction?"

In the English language, with its millions of words, terms, and an overemphasis on nuance, there is a tendency to get hung up on fine points and on deconstructing terms.

Creative nonfiction – a form that has existed perhaps as long as writing itself – is a genre that incorporates the principles of journalism with the drama and color normally associated with fiction. It is quite simply putting an interesting and compelling spin on telling a true story.

Too often, rule-makers convey the sense to writers that if something is fact-based it must be limited to telling who, what, where, when, why, and how devoid of humor and drama that is not inherent to the story .

Nonsense.

While it's true that most informative news stories are not generally considered entertaining, that goes back to the issue of parsing words and of confusing tone with content. Reality can be funny, and, at times, highly original.

Early histories and tales from far-off lands, when well-told, gave us the excitement of discovery and learning something new.

More recently, Ernest Hemingway wrote about a bullfight, detailing all the excitement and drama of the event, including the speed, grace, strength, and courage of the participants, while neither fabricating nor exaggerating a single word of the account.

It was all true, yet represented with the color and drama intact, much as a short story would have been had the event not actually taken place.

Creative nonfiction should not be confused with the "historical novel" – a fictional work set in an actual time and place and involving people who really existed.

Truman Capote's powerful book *In Cold Blood*, which tells the story of a Kansas family's murder in chilling detail, is not an example of creative nonfiction because that book also includes the author's impressions of participants in the story and what they might have been thinking or feeling at various times. Though the people were real, the story's perspective was based on opinion, not fact. It was more in the area of "the new journalism," which we covered a while ago.

Lee Gutkind, a professor of English at the University of Pittsburgh, has been a strong proponent and teacher of creative nonfiction, conducting workshops and presenting readings in the genre, which he considers good, old-fashioned reporting plus insight, story, reflection... and wisdom.

Consider a survivor of a plane crash or a rockslide or a hijacking or a kidnapping, telling the story and providing a vivid picture without exaggeration, making listeners and readers feel they can connect with events and understand what the experience must have been like. Creative nonfiction is writing such true stories about people in ways that may seem odd, interesting, funny, poignant, sad, or sweet. The writer, though not a participant in the event, can present the story with the same details, facts, accuracy, sensitivity, and emotion. That's creative nonfiction and, by any measure, writing worth reading.

The form requires research and reflection, which both allows and encourages the writer to adhere to journalistic principles, yet avoid the detached perspective that produces dry and lifeless – though accurate – reporting. The writer becomes a fly on the wall recounting events in third-person – not injecting himself or herself into the story, but bringing the reader closer to the occurrence. Creative nonfiction allows readers to get close enough to the story to appreciate what it feels like to be there without being there, with the writer as driver and true storyteller.

Good writing is supposed to evoke sensation in the reader.
Not the fact that it is raining, but the feeling of being rained upon.
— **E.L. Doctorow**

The writer who cares more about words than about story –
characters, action, setting, atmosphere – is unlikely to create a vivid and
continuous dream; he gets in his own way too much; in his poetic drunk-
enness, he can't tell the cart – and its cargo – from the horse.
— **John Gardner**

A Writing Exercise

1. Reflect briefly on events in your life.

2. List what you believe are the five most important days or events you've lived through.

3. Choose one event from the list and write about it in no more than 750 words (about three double-spaced pages).

4. Apply the journalistic rules, noting who, what, when, where, and why.

5. Edit your story, checking to make certain it is totally factual.

6. Reread the story, imagining it as fiction. What added elements of color, energy, or excitement might you add?

7. Revise the story, making certain you're added touches that are true. Opinions, dialog, and quotations can be inserted into the story, as long as they are identified as such and clearly attributed.

Part Two:

Topics

Topics: An Overview

Part One of this book presented forty essays on writing with exercises that show how the ideas and theories could be applied. Part Two takes a closer, more in-depth look at fifteen of the topics discussed in the essays. Specific aspects of public relations writing, advertising, research, grammar, style, form, media, and the writing process itself are considered, with additional information on topics often overlooked by writers.

Creating good writing is not magic; but it sometimes seems that way.

Is it possible to teach someone to be a good writer? Well, yes and no. As with most subjects, agreement is not a foregone conclusion. In earlier years we provided elementary school introductions to the alphabet, printing big, clear capitol and small letters (which later grow up to be called upper and lower case) with a number-two pencil, and learning cursive handwriting.

And, of course, we all learned to type (even though I love my pen). Fortunately, we received some very good advice way back when. The Greek philosopher and teacher Epictetus, more than 2,000 years ago in Rome, wrote, "If you wish to be a writer, write." By the way, it also sounds good in Greek and Latin.

Elsewhere in this book, you'll find several variations on this theme of learning by doing. People learn to write by writing, re-writing, and then rewriting their rewrites. Few complete examples of good writing are found in first drafts, though you can often see small sparkling moments. The idea may be there and much of the best raw material that will end up in a final version may be there, but like a diamond that needs polishing to bring out its best, new writing usually needs polishing to make it good writing. Some writing programs devote a disproportionately long time to theory and less time putting words on paper.

Writers find inspiration in what they see and hear, but, more often, from what they read. If some writing seems a bit derivative, it's probably because it is. It's not unusual for writers to read something and react with a feeling that it was good, but could have been better and go on to use that as inspiration for a new or adapted version.

For example, Pulitzer Prize winner James Kirkwood once said he enjoyed John Knowles' novel *A Separate Peace...* but thought he could have written it better. He may have been only half-joking. Then again, he went on to write *Good Times/Bad Times*, a fictionalized story of an episode in his own life that had many similarities to the Knowles book. Whether Kirkwood wrote a better book could be a subject for debate, but it would not be the only time a writer was inspired or motivated to write something after reading another writer's work.

Best selling novelist T.C. Boyle, who is also an English professor at the University of Southern California, addressed the question of whether or not it is possible to teach someone to be a good writer.

"No," he answered, then added, "Well, to be a competent writer, sure. But not to be a great writer. You must have a great talent to be a great writer... My purpose in my students' lives is to be their coach, just as I was coached by others – not taught, necessarily. You're taught by other writers by reading their books."

Mr. Boyle saw himself as a coach and Kurt Vonnegut, in his years teaching at the University of Iowa's Writers Workshop, likened himself to a golf pro who didn't expect to make his pupils great golfers, but hoped to help them shave a few strokes off their games. Other writers have offered some observations worth reading:

- William Zinsser, a distinguished writer and editor who also teaches at the New School in New York, famously wrote, "Writing is thinking on paper."

- According to novelist Gabriel Fielding, "The mere habit of writing, of constantly keeping at it, of never giving up, ultimately teaches you how to write."

- Journalist Richard Harding Davis believes, "The secret of good writing is to say an old thing in a new way or to say a new thing in an old way."

- Tobias Wolff wrote, "To be a writer, you have to be a reader. And you have to be a ravenous reader, an addict, a fiend."

- "New writers are often told, 'Write what you know,'" wrote author Marjorie Franco. "I would broaden that by saying, write what you know emotionally."

- Then again, Novelist Donna Tartt believes, "The worst advice is to write about what you know. It's hard to see things fresh."

- Or how's this? Grace Paley suggested, "Write from what you know into what you don't know."

Such comments indicate that many writers are often asked how they do what they do, and they have very definite ideas about writing – about how it should be taught, how it's learned, what it should say, and how it should – or shouldn't – be read. This book contains my definite ideas.

These pages reflect many ideas and opinions, along with standards, rules, guidelines, commentary, and very few exclamation points.

The content is designed to introduce you to how it feels to write for specific audiences, as well as for the general public, through both direct written communication and through the mass media. It's fairly comprehensive, but we won't go into depth.

Sections on Writing for Advertising and Writing for Public Relations, as well as on Speechwriting, offer basic forms and formats of these genres. How to create effective print and broadcast copy, brochures, direct mail, press releases, and Internet communications are all addressed as well.

Entire books have been written on all of these as areas of specialization. This is like a series of sampler plates, it's not a complete meal. So if you wish to pursue any of these specialties further, more good advice awaits in many other books. Occasionally, we've listed a few, but, since that list changes daily, you're as well off going to Google or your favorite bookstore – new or used. But whatever specialty you pursue, here is a point worth remembering. Good writing is good writing. It is only the vehicles, format or venue that change.

I have been successful probably because I have always realized that
I knew nothing about writing and have merely tried
to tell an interesting story entertainingly.
— **Edgar Rice Burroughs**

Topic 1: Grammar and Style

Grammar is the way sentences in a language are constructed.

It's more than mechanics, but not a lot more. Even if you want to – for good reason – violate some of the rules of grammar, it's best that you know them before you break them. T.S. Eliot knew a few things about good writing. It was Eliot who wrote "it's not wise to violate the rules until you know how to observe them."

Style? Now it gets interesting. Last time I looked, style had more than 20 definitions and probably as many specific examples as there are writers with style.

One more thing. Grammar and style are completely intertwined.

The short to-the-point sentences of a classic like Hemingway or a pop novelist like James Patterson (you may or may not like him, but he certainly has a style) have a very basic relationship with the rules of grammar.

Meanwhile, the more elegant style, adding a subordinate clause to make an interesting point, and then adding one more for a richer reading experience, a style that I happen to prefer, needs just a bit more attention to the rules of grammar so that the reader is able to exit the sentence that he or she enters – without getting lost along the way. Did you follow that?

Grammar

In writing, the rules should begin with an understanding of the mechanics of the English language – of grammar and sentence structure. We repeat. "Grammar is the way sentences in a language are constructed."

Writers must know that *nouns* are names of things, places, and people and *verbs* are action words that describe what's going on with the nouns. *Adjectives* describe nouns, *adverbs* describe verbs. A *sentence* is a group of words that usually contain a single thought or point. A *paragraph* is generally a group of sentences that expand upon that point, providing more information or detail.

Punctuation marks keep those building blocks organized. After that, it's up to you. Build your sentences long or short. The rat-a-tat of short sentences, punctuated by plenty of periods. Or the more extended rhythm of writing that takes its time to describe a scene or a concept, with comma-laden clauses.

If you are quite clear about what you are doing, you can, perhaps, invent a word or two, like Roald Dahl who has a quizzalicious way of making up an almost word that gives his writing a unique flavor. And, in our popular culture, we also create or mutate words all the time – turning nouns into verbs, for example. Now, to "concept" may be the act of coming up with concepts – a verb – as well as the thing that is the result – the noun. But, even so, the mechanical rules apply.

There is one more resource that I believe is pretty much required on every writer's desk or bookshelf - a copy of *The Elements of Style* by Strunk and White. This thin volume, continuously in print since 1918, is not only an excellent guide and reference, but is, and has been, a source of simple yet powerful wisdom for generations of writers.

As rules go, consider this:

A sentence should contain no unnecessary words, a paragraph no unnecessary sentences, for the same reason that a drawing should have no unnecessary lines and a machine no unnecessary parts.

Ninety years after it was written, that sentence says more than some books, and many large books have been written that should have paid attention to this small one.

If your fate involves a certain amount of technical or business writing, you may need another resource or two. For more information (on subjects, predicates, infinitive phrases, adverbial phrases, subordinating and correlative conjunctions, dependent clauses, participles, etc.), I'd recommend the *Handbook of Business English*.

It is also worth noting that some very learned and excellent writers will intentionally violate rules of good grammar. Their reasons may vary, but it works for them. I still treasure the quote used earlier from Winston Churchill as he told a woman overly concerned with grammar, "Madam, this is the sort of nonsense up with I shall not put." But, again, Mr. Churchill knew the rule he chose to break.

Know the rules. Writers with a good command of grammar will be able to communicate more effectively whether they choose to obey those rules or not.

Style
The term style has two applications in writing: (1) the format or "rules" that guide the written presentation, and (2) the tone of a written work that could be described as either original or derivative.

Some aspects of what people term "style" is actually being grammatical. And, some styles can be achieved by purposely breaking those rules. Here are two examples. Mark Twain's *Huckleberry Finn* achieved a certain narrative character when Twain deliberately built the voice of Huck with an unsophisticated grammar and vocabulary. Today, advertising copywriters, whether they wish to cut their copy to fit into a short format, or just "punch up" their copy, will often use sentence fragments. Those are just two examples. But they are purposeful, not accidental.

Other forms and styles are quite purposeful in following certain forms and formats, especially newspaper writing, though it is also required for managing the content of reports, theses, dissertations, and white papers.

The result is the stylebook or style guide, most commonly the *AP Style Guide*. Its official name is the *Associated Press Stylebook and Libel Manual*. This is the reference work to fall back on when in doubt about the proper use of titles, abbreviations, case, number usage, punctuation, and other technical or structural standards. Alternate sources cited with some frequency include the *University of Chicago Manual of Style* and the *Style Guide of the American Psychological Association*.

So that's pretty much it for the official versions of proper writing style. As with other official controlling authorities, writers grant themselves exceptions from established formats when they believe the content requires such departure or when their creative prerogatives trump rules. This is often the case when writing for the Internet, which many writers continue to view as an untamed frontier of sorts where anything goes, including that perversion of spelling brought about by texting. Grl, LOL, BTW, etc.

The second application of style can involve nonfiction, but more often relates to fiction, poetry, sci-fi, advertising copy, and such works where the word creative is invoked to justify whatever a writer chooses to do. In these areas, a "creative writer" might become excited about the prospect of breaking rules as a way of validating creativity or uniqueness.

Nonsense. Notable creative writers with reputations for edgy, irreverent, cutting-edge/outside-the-box/choose-your-own-cliché writing – Thomas Pynchon, Tom Robbins, and Dave Eggers come to mind – are in fact disciplined and educated writers who understand editing and literary nuance. Their work is in fact far from the wacky, first draft, stream-of-consciousness material it appears to be.

Though it may seem that many creative writers do some of their best work having thrown the style guide to the winds, there is, in most cases, a very conscious process that created those styles. For example, Charles Bukowski, a true maverick-writer of both poetry and prose, claimed Chekhov, Kafka, Dostoyevsky, and D.H. Lawrence among his greatest literary influences.

Do you have a style you like? When it comes to style, writers typically start out imitating writers they admire and enjoy reading. This is not only common, but is a very positive way to develop a comfortable style of your own. Whether or not imitation is the sincerest form of flattery, it's a good way to find your own personal writing rhythm.

In the beginning, I believe a writer should experiment, trying on different styles of writing, different rhythmic approaches, and taking on different subjects. And to quote again Winston Churchill, "Short words are best and the old words when short are best of all."

One of the really bad things you can do to your writing is to
dress up the vocabulary, looking for long words because you're
maybe a little bit ashamed of your short ones.
— **Stephen King**

Next to doing things that deserve to be written,
nothing gets a man more credit, or gives him more pleasure
than to write things that deserve to be read.
— **Lord Chesterfield**

It is perfectly okay to write garbage –
as long as you edit brilliantly.
— **C. J. Cherryh**

Exercises:

Let's stretch our style muscles. Consider the following:

Let the reader know what you are trying to say.

A sentence should contain no unnecessary words, a paragraph no unnecessary sentences, for the same reason that a drawing should have no unnecessary lines and a machine no unnecessary parts.

- Write a 200-word journal entry explaining why you want to write and what you want to write.

- After completing your journal entry, go back and circle all the nouns and underline all the verbs.

- Consider what other nouns and verbs might have been used in their places to let the reader know what you are trying to say more clearly, interestingly, or dramatically.

- Now look at the rhythm of your writing. Is that, in general, "your personal writing rhythm?" You're probably not sure. So let's try this.

- Now, take the same entry and see how punchy you can make it. Short to-the-point sentences. Cut your 200 word piece down to the bone.

- Now let's do the opposite. Pretend you're being paid by the word. Add descriptive phrases as much as you can, without your writing completely falling apart from clause and comma overload. Try to keep to a fairly well-patterned rhythm.

- Now think about it. Some of you may instantly discover your personal writing rhythm. For most of us, it's an ongoing process and you'll be dialing that rhythm up and down depending on the feel of the writing you want to do and the nature of the assignment.

- Here's the good news. Something new has happened to you. You've started to become aware of developing your own writing rhythm.

Topic 2: The Planning Process

How do writers write?

The short answer is any way they can. The alternative response is to have a plan, and that can take longer – in some cases, perhaps a lifetime. To be more specific, as with so many questions regarding the process of writing, there is no single answer because there are as many possibilities as there are writers.

However, there is a range of planning approaches and, as a beginning writer, it will be helpful to understand that range and perhaps sample a few – to find what works best for you.

In fact, you may very well find that you develop a range that matches up with the type of writing you are doing at the time.

Here are some examples.

The specific assignment – length, topic, and deadline are clearly established. News writers receive assignments or submit ideas that must be approved by an editor, who then may establish parameters of what can be in the story or what must be in the story, as well as its length and deadline. The writer might then conduct research, check sources, interview witnesses, locate experts, and identify or eliminate persons who might have information or something to add, verify content, check facts, and work through several drafts before the story is turned in (filed) and appears in print or as part of a broadcast or news program.

Newswriting. Regular newswriting jobs often have fairly clear guidelines that are useful for generating regular consistent written material.

- A writer on a beat might be expected to file a story (or several stories) a day.

- Business reporters file market updates and commentary several times an hour.

- A crime reporter might be covering a trial and provide information at regular intervals or when important developments occur for the span of the trial, which could be a few days or a year or longer.

Feature writing. Feature writing, as you might imagine, has a wider range of planning approaches.

- A magazine writer, depending on the closing dates and publication schedule of the magazine, might have a story in each issue – weekly, monthly, quarterly – or might be allowed "as long as it takes" to fully develop an important story.

Other types of writing.

- At the other extreme are types of writing that may involve a very lengthy process.

  For example, people who follow events or occurrences (astronomic or archeological, for example) for years – even decades – before acquiring the information or witnessing the event that is the subject or substance of a story.

  In the same vein, academic articles, written for specialized journals, with a certain commonly accepted "academic style" have their own process. They often go through "peer review" where the article is examined and criticized by others with expertise in the field.

Planning is not something that requires an MBA. Typically plans involve an initial stage of information gathering or idea generation, some sort of first draft, and then polishing into the final form. Pretty simple.

As to the amount of time involved at each stage, here is where my observation that it varies widely is demonstrated in almost infinite variety. Some projects come to us in a blinding flash of inspiration and seem to complete themselves almost effortlessly. Others seem to demand that every syllable have a bit of blood or sweat (sometimes both) invested in the outcome.

That said, here are a few tips:

- **Think.** Planning begins with thinking. If that sounds more than a little simplistic, consider this: Whether writing a biography, an autobiography, a collection of poems or thoughts, a journal, a novel, or *Readers' Digest* favorite topics, such as "My most unforgettable character" or "How I spent My Summer Vacation," virtually all writing plans follow similar processes.

- **Keep notes.** A folder (one of many) for collecting material on the topic is usually a good idea, a notebook, a journal, paper napkins, quick entries on a computer notebook handheld word processor, or on a long roll of wrapping paper (that's how Jack Kerouac wrote *On the Road* with a jazz album playing while he typed... It doesn't matter when or where, the intellectual raw material for your project – present or future – needs to be noted and saved.

- **Make lists.** Lists are a reflection of organization and of approaching subjects with a more strategic outlook. You may be surprised at how simply re-doing a list you've done before gives you a new insight, new connection, or new organizational approach on the material you're working with. It happens to me often.

- **Organize and re-organize**. I keep stirring and re-stirring the pot – it works for me. Organize your notes into a readable, manageable series of points (like these) or a series of pages – one idea or topic per page – and review what you have, prioritize your points according to good/better/best/ save for another time/ and what was I thinking?

Organizing and planning are companion terms.

It is hard to plan with a cluttered file, desk, or mind. And, since most of us have a bit of clutter in one or all of these places, a bit of straightening up – both physical and mental – tends to have a positive result.

As with people in many professions, writers enjoy discussing what they do, with the exception of J.D. Salinger and some others who insist on maintaining their privacy and perhaps a sense of mystery about their craft, preferring to let the writing speak for itself.

To know is nothing at all; to imagine is everything.
— **Anatole France**

My aim is to put down what I see and what I feel
in the best and simplest way I can tell it.
— **Ernest Hemingway**

Topic 3: The Creative Process

Writers learn fairly quickly the expression "beauty is in the eye of the beholder" is not only true, but that it applies to a great deal more than just beauty. So much in life is subjective, from people's choices of food, the clothes they wear, reading material, music, art, who they find attractive, what colors they prefer, etc. The entire issue of choice is about what people know or discover they need or like, don't like, or find beautiful. In society, what is in the eye of the beholder is often overlooked when broad judgments are made.

A 2006 Pew Research Study found that 90 percent of Americans believe other Americans are overweight, but only 40 percent of respondents believed they were themselves overweight. Surveys also indicate that a majority of people consider themselves to be creative in some way. This comment is almost certain to raise eyebrows. With all that creativity, why does so much of what is produced seem so derivative – so lacking in originality? Perhaps creativity, like beauty, is in the eye of the beholder.

In broad terms, the creative process involves generating new ideas or concepts or new adaptations between existing ideas or concepts using imagination, critical thinking, employing problem-solving skills, and an ability to reflect on the finished product.

To approach an assignment with creativity, a writer must trust his or her intuition. Ideas are everywhere and the creative process can involve brainstorming, groups of like or unlike minds bouncing ideas off of one another, intensely studying something in hopes of finding some new application or characteristic of it, meditating...

The *American Heritage Dictionary* defines creative writing as characterized by originality and expressiveness; imaginative. For some people creativity is putting the same characters in a different location to see how they will react. Or reversing the roles.

As ideas are formed, write them down. Visualize how the execution of the ideas might look. The creative process involves following through on ideas to see where they might go.

Dr. R. S. Nickerson, in *Enhancing Creativity*, provides a summary of 12 proposed techniques, including approaches developed by members of both the business and academic communities:

1. Establish purpose and intention.
2. Build basic skills.
3. Encourage acquisitions of domain-specific knowledge.
4. Stimulate and reward curiosity and exploration.
5. Build motivation, especially internal motivation.
6. Encourage confidence and a willingness to take risks.
7. Focus on mastery and self-competition.
8. Promote supportable beliefs about creativity.
9. Provide opportunities for choice and discovery.
10. Develop self-management (metacognitive skills).
11. Teach techniques and strategies for facilitating creative performance.
12. Provide balance.

Every day writers read, whether they are aware of it or not, from books and newspapers to labels on packaging, instruction manuals or a variety of lists. Reading gives rise to inspiration and an analysis of most written material opens up the possibilities. Again, the best approach to the creative process is the one that works for the writer. Try different techniques, including using ideas that have been used before, imagining if their execution had been handled differently, and asking... what if?

- Take deep breaths. Relax. This is not a meditation exercise (although it can be). It's difficult to be creative with a closed mind and excessive stress.

- Stop/Look/Listen. This seems like advice that is better dispensed set to music in a preschool class, but it's the real deal. Life happens quickly.

  - Pause to notice it. There is much to be learned.

  - Observing is a learned skill. The expression to look, but not see is not simply a phrase, it describes reality. What is unseen is missed and that can be costly to a writer. People tend to be familiar with the concept of listening skills, but not with the practice.

  - Listening is not only a skill that could probably benefit people in most situations, it can provide unique advantages and surprises for writers. The content of what is said, how it is said, what it means, and what is left unsaid can speak volumes.

Decide what you want to write… or don't. If you have a clear idea about what you want to write (or, in the case of an assignment, what you need to write), review what notes and ideas you have and begin outlining what you have and making notes as to what you need to fill in any gaps.

If you do not have a clear focus, begin putting words – any words – on paper (or on a screen) and allow a stream of consciousness to gather momentum… write a name or a date or a place and open your mind to what you associate with those words. After a few minutes of this, it is likely something approaching a germ of an idea to build upon will emerge. Don't force it; just let the words come. There are enough words, thoughts, ideas, experiences, and references inside people that something interesting will emerge if it is allowed to do so.

Topic 4: The Writing Process

How many different ways can we say that it varies? Writers can be informal, freewheeling, rigid, dogmatic, focused, diligent, detail-oriented, flippant, or any combination of those characteristics and several others. It has been said that no two writers or authors follow the same process in getting their words from conception to page (or to the computer screen, as the case may be). That may be either an overstatement or overly simplistic. It varies. The point is that, just as writers' finished work may reflect many different influences and styles, the process of initiating and completing the work can employ different steps, rituals, and styles as well.

Throughout this book references are made to technique – to how writers work. Sometimes a particular process or system for producing content is mandatory. A newspaper's newsroom or a weekly or monthly magazine, a TV or radio station, or a Web site committed to scheduled reports or updates, for example, require structure and organization to operate efficiently. Every person going his or her own way is contrary to the concept of organization or of operating as a team. These are situations where a process is imposed on the writer. But even within most formal processes, there is room for individuals to find a comfort level that allows each person to function effectively and satisfactorily.

Writers, because of the unique, personal, often creative aspect of the job, need to find the working styles that work best for them, inside or outside of an organizational structure. The general rule is that whatever approach works best for the writer is the correct approach, but that doesn't mean structure and discipline don't count. It's important that the writer understand that even the most creative work under liberal conditions requires discipline and attention to detail.

In *Strategic Writing*, a popular volume by Marsh, Guth and Short, the recommended approach to the writing process involves nine seemingly self-explanatory steps:

1. Research
2. Creativity/Brainstorming
3. Organizing/Outlining
4. Writing
5. Revision
6. Editing
7. Seeking Approval
8. Distribution
9. Evaluation

While this process appears straightforward enough, some writing coaches or instructors might argue with the order in which the steps are listed. Why not edit the work before revising it? Perhaps research should come after brainstorming so the results of the brainstorming session can be tested against the research data, etc. Should number 4 in the writing process be writing or isn't that inherently part of the entire process? And how many different ways can we say that it varies?

Depending on the particular mentor, instructor, coach, facilitator, course, or guidelines, the logical or obvious or simple steps may seem either more or less simple than the list suggests.

The approach of the Writing Center at Cleveland State University draws upon another resource, the *Allyn & Bacon Handbook*, and recommends the writing process follow a very different nine-step process that includes:

1. Invention Technique
2. Critical Reading
3. Thesis

4. Organization

5. Paragraphing

6. Word-Processing

7. Revision

8. Documentation

9. Proofreading

Note that the only step on both lists is the one that deals with the issue of organizing material. Some of the terms, such as Invention Technique, a term that requires some explanation, involve reading, brainstorming, journalist's questioning (asking who, what, when, where, why, and how), journal writing, free-writing, mapping, and the many parts strategy, and steps that are ongoing and exist outside of the writing process.

Critical reading means applying certain factors, models, questions, and theories that result in enhanced clarity and comprehension; the Thesis Statement outlines the central purpose of the writing. Simply put, Organization is about arranging thoughts in an orderly and functional way; paragraphing involves arranging the sections of the writing in groups of sentences related to each other because they all refer to the controlling idea established by the thesis. Word-processing writing, obviously, refers to the role of the computer as a tool to facilitate production of the written work. The word processor is the successor to the typewriter, which replaced the ballpoint pen. That, in turn, has its ancestry in quills made from the feathers of eagles that many writers wish were still used, particularly when printers break down. Then again, I'm told that the eagles are much happier and consider it progress long overdue.

Revision in writing may apply to changes that alter the meaning or organization of a text or changes that may leave meaning intact, but alter the wording. (And should I leave in the eagle joke?) Documentation relates to citing source. Proofreading, which could also be considered a part of the revision process, reminds the writer that spelling and grammar still count.

MIT's writing center recommends a four-step writing process that includes pre-writing, drafting, revising, and editing. Presumably, the steps in other lists that covered the mapping and paragraphing, etc., are somewhere within the four-step approach that MIT advocates.

While the processes are varied, no one approach is the one that fits every writer's size and shape. And, of course, different assignments each imply their own variations on the planning process. Some of the lists refer to pre-writing, which can include any activity a writer performs before actually writing a draft of an article, essay, document, or whatever the project entails. Pre-writing activities might include thinking, taking notes, discussing the assignment or project, brainstorming, outlining, or gathering information by means of interviewing people, accessing library materials for research, or assessing data. Creating a draft of the writing follows.

Pre-writing is very much a catch-all term, as "thinking" and "taking notes" are not inherently a part of the writing process, but are parts of life. But for writers to focus on what they are doing inside and outside of the process has value and taking observation and listening skills to a higher level will be in no way detrimental to that process.

At the University of Wisconsin at Madison's Writing Center the writing process includes these steps:

- Planning to write
- Creating an argument
- Working with sources
- Drafting and revising the work, and
- Finishing the paper.

Again, not much explanation is required and the steps reflect other noted approaches, albeit by different names. Planning to Write, a step that largely focuses on reading material to be reviewed as a writing exercise; Creating an Argument, which is stating and proving a thesis; Working with Sources, quoting, attributing, and paraphrasing; Drafting and Revising the Work using peer reviews; and Finishing the Paper, which examines the paper against an editing checklist, before proofreading.

What an examination of the writing process and its various approaches proves is that writers recognize there are different ways to write and, whether the ways or their descriptions include pre-writing, mapping, paragraphing, critical reading, or other possibly esoteric terms, writing is still about the words. But the writers of those words need to be organized.

The terms are not as important as finding a system that works for you and produces the desired result. Research is relevant to any type of writing any time, simply because research eliminates, or at least minimizes, errors.

Whether the process begins in the morning and lasts all day or follows a rigid and disciplined schedule of hours or days, keeping the writing simple, and concise, knowing the audience for the writing, and editing and proofreading for errors shows a respect for the reader and a sense of professionalism on the part of the writer.

There is no single process that is the right process for every journalist, poet, novelist, or business writer. That's why a roomful of writers could all be writing on the same subject and the resulting work will show distinct differences. So, while there is no one way, every writer needs to find their own way. Some of these may help you do that.

Topic 5: Long Form, Short Form, Free Form…

Pamphlets, Columns, Articles, Stories, Books

Good writing is good writing. Writers come up with lines like that all the time – a simplistic take that appears to incorporate wisdom and philosophy, with just a bit of redundancy. It is a truth that explains itself without seeming to say anything, yet it says a great deal. What it says is that, regardless of the form, length, category, or genre – from an advertising slogan or the teaser line on the outside of a direct mail envelope to the most expansive historical epic, novel or dissertation – a writer who can understand and apply the principles of good writing can write anything, regardless of its length, form, or function.

Whatever the format or medium, how do writers write? That question may also seem absurdly simplistic, as have been many of the attempts to answer it. Whether early in the morning, only on weekends, or at night when the phone stops ringing (with the exception of cell phones, which seem to never require sleep); whether with a large quill pen or a small notebook computer, the shortest, truest answer is writers write however they can. More seriously, a good response is writing is like simply talking – saying something – without speaking. It is thinking on a page or screen. The theory holds that if a person can think or speak, that person can write. It's the editing of what ends up on the paper that may need some fine-tuning.

The most fortunate writers choose their venues. Some don't. Writers who want to earn a living rarely manage to land good paying jobs until they have acquired considerable experience (or a few lucky breaks). The dream of many young writers, to launch their careers with a best-selling book, alas, remains just a dream for most of them. Writing a book, finding an agent, closing a deal, receiving a large advance and getting continued large royalty checks actually does happen to some, but the percentages are similar to those of having a winning lottery ticket. But writers who care only about writing find opportunities do exist and they can be extremely satisfying in every sense of the word.

There is a market today for "long form" pieces of the type that routinely appear in magazines, such as the *New Yorker* or *Vanity Fair*. "Short form" writing could be product descriptions in catalogs, short films, TV or music reviews for a newspaper or magazine "calendar" section; trade magazines and newsletters published weekly, monthly, or quarterly for virtually every profession and industry; or the proliferation of cable and satellite TV channels, Internet sites, YouTube, and podcasts, which have opened a plethora of outlets for seasoned or aspiring writers.

Writing can be divided into the two primary categories, fiction and nonfiction, but within those categories, subcategories abound, such as Creative Writing, which has as its primary purpose to entertain and attempt to create an emotional response or connection, through humor, fantasy, poetry, promotions, or other types of storytelling or narrative; Business Writing that focuses on commercial, financial, or organization-related issues of interest to investors, employees, and specific segments of the public; Expository Writing that provides information, explanation, or direction; Persuasive Writing, which presents an opinion and attempts to influence the reader into supporting a position, and numerous other interest-related fields.

The writing's form and function might include any or all of these types of writing:

- An abstract
- Advertising
- Article

- Copy
- Autobiography
- Backgrounder
- Bills (as in a laws, not invoices)
- Biography
- Blogs
- Brochure
- Column
- Comic book
- Comic strip
- Fact sheet
- Flyer
- Grant
- Internet postings
- Letter
- Mission statement
- Newspaper
- Newsletter
- Notes
- Novel
- Pamphlets
- Plan
- Play
- Press release
- Profile
- Proposal
- Public service announcement
- Report
- Research
- Résumé
- Review
- Screenplay
- Short story
- Speech
- Story

- Storyboard
- Study
- White paper

While any or all of the above (and others) have what could be termed "standard" length and presentation formats, nothing is fixed in stone. For printing purposes some publications still determine length according to a "signature" (the assembled pages and images of a publication, as printed on a single large sheet of paper before trimming is called a "form" and when the pages of a form are in correct order, after folding and trimming, the form becomes a signature of usually eight or sixteen pages). Today, lengths vary widely. A magazine article can be 30 or more pages; a book can be 80 or 800. A monograph can, like a book, be short or long.

When someone thinks of a pamphlet today, the allusion is typically to a small brochure that explains hair loss or cholesterol levels, tips on ways to conserve electrical energy, or a brief message about religious beliefs. But that was not always the case. A pamphlet is an unbound booklet, usually a single, folded sheet of paper printed on both sides that has a place in history. A pamphleteer would create and distribute pamphlets to try to persuade people to vote for a certain politician or support a particular political ideology. One of the most famous pamphleteers was the American Revolutionary War hero Thomas Paine. That alone should be enough to make some people rethink their opinions about the inconsequential nature of pamphlets. And perhaps the role of public relations tools as well.

Newspapers might still limit the length of columns and specific publications will provide longer or shorter articles or stories according to their stated missions to do so.

Regardless of the form or format, a good starting point for a writer is to ask:

- What's the primary purpose of the writing?

- What are possible secondary purposes?
- Who is the audience?
- What assumptions about the audience does the writer need to know?
- What is the logic behind the written presentation?
- What information is required for each section?
- Does the writer need to adopt a particular language, style, or tone the reader will expect from this piece?
- Is this a "stand alone" writing project or part of a series or campaign?
- Who or what is the writer's primary source for information?
- What legal or regulatory information, if any, needs to be included or cited?

Whatever the length or venue, writers become confident relatively quickly and come to appreciate that good writing is good writing.

Newspapers cannot be defined by the second word – paper.
They've got to be defined by the first word – news.
— **New York Times publisher Arthur O. Sulzberg, Jr.**

I think I did pretty well,
considering I started out with nothing but a bunch of blank paper.
— **Steve Martin**

Writing is its own reward.
— **Henry Miller**

Topic 6: Words and Terms... and Loving Writing

When the evil Lord Voldemort wiped out everyone in sight, the only survivor was the baby Harry Potter, who not only went on to heroically do battle with the Dark Lord years later, but to be the driving force in a seven-book series that, between 1997 and 2007, sold more than 340 million copies. But commercial success notwithstanding, what was it that kept Baby Harry alive when all around him had succumbed?

It was love.

Readers of the Harry Potter books know that at the time of her death, Harry's mother passed to her child her own magical powers and such a mega-dose of love, he was not only able to deflect the evil Voldemort's attack, but to send him off into an other-worldly state of darkness that even the Energizer Bunny couldn't generate enough power to light the way back. It was the Power of Love. In the words of a 1965 song, "Funny What Love Can Do."

Love saved a young boy's life and was the catalyst in getting tens of millions of children and many of their parents reading books at a time of extreme video game obsession, when people seemed to have given up on books. Love is a good word. It enables Hallmark to sell greeting cards to people who spend endless hours staring at computer screens. Love is not the same when read from a computer screen as it is from a card.

A greeting card – an odd idea, handing someone a written message of love, friendship, good wishes, or sorrow, or a joke coming from one person, but written by someone else. Yet, as if by proxy, the writer of the words on the card is writing on behalf of the giver of the card. The sentiment is duly noted; Happy Birthday; Happy Anniversary; Get Well Soon; My Sincerest Condolences; Congratulations on Your Engagement/New Job/New Home/New Baby/Marriage; Merry Christmas. The transfer is successful. Words did it.

Lewis Burke Frumkes, the editor of the *Logophile's Orgy*, sent out hundreds of letters asking writers, scientists, educators, entertainers, and celebrities of every stripe to tell him their favorite word and why that's the case. More than 200 responded, including Dr. Linus Pauling, advice columnist Ann Landers, editor Lewis Lapham, filmmaker Roman Polanski, writers Norman Mailer, Dave Barry, Amy Tan, Mary Higgins Clark, and Ray Bradbury, singer Gloria Estafan, actress Hedy Lamarr, sports columnist Ira Berkow, and many more. Their words were interesting to read – words most people probably never think about:

- Ramshackle
- Hottentot
- Iguana
- Oneiric
- Resplendent
- Wonderful
- Festoon
- Silence
- Hermeneutics
- Skidsomycetees
- Windowsill
- Oolitic limestone
- Dilatory
- Yogurt
- Exquisite
- Mongolia
- Virility
- Empathy
- Mama

- Choice
- Option
- Autumn
- Modulate
- Promulgate

Many respondents reported they liked their words simply because of how they sounded rolling off their tongues; others because of what the words symbolized to them – power, strength, or emotional well-being. Many of the words were gross or obscene, but it was interesting to read the person's often quite intellectually stated explanation of how it came to be his or her choice.

From bamboozle and egg to cornucopia and, again, love, famous people share words that matter to them in a fascinating exercise because many people, until they were asked, did not even realize they had a favorite word.

From what goes into the love letters, sacred vows, the words on the trophy, or a last will and testament, words become more than simply a means of communicating, they represent dreams and promises.

Love is a good word. So is sex. People respond immediately when they see either word written. One would think that after all this time people would have no need to check their dictionaries for the meaning of love (or sex), but, according to the online publisher of Dictionary.com, they were once again two of the most sought out words in 2005. Here is a list of the most searched for words for each letter of the alphabet:

affect
benevolent
cynical
definitely
effect
fallacious
gregarious

hyperbole
irony
jaded
karma
love
metaphor
naive
oxymoron
paradox
quixotic
rhetoric
sex
theme
ubiquitous
virtue
whether
xenophobia
yield
zeal

One writer described her passion for writing and words this way:

My love of writing comes from the power it gives me to be the direc-tor of my own movie, using the page as my movie screen. When I write, it's as if I'm watching pictures on a screen parade before my eyes, and the picture that you, the reader, see is all up to me... How could anyone not love this power that is entrusted to those who pick up the pen?

Power. There's an interesting word to apply to a writer. Most writers probably don't feel all-powerful; rather more like storytell-ers, painting pictures with words and trying to make the images in the pictures move.

The writer William Zinsser raised an interesting point in his book *On Writing Well*. The word pictures writers paint also have sound.

"Bear in mind, when you're choosing words and stringing them together, how they sound," Zinsser wrote. "This may seem absurd: readers read with their eyes. But in fact they hear what they are reading far more than you realize. Therefore such matters as rhythm and alliteration are vital to every sentence."

Whether writers see themselves as directors, storytellers, powerful supernatural overlords, incurable romantics, or simply presenters of information, the words provide strength no energy drink or hours at a gym can produce. And maybe a bit of magic as well.

While tight with concentration on what is being written,
the writer has a thought, an insight, a partially articulate concept.
The natural response is to think, "I can't stop what I am writing.
I'll remember the idea," and continue writing. The writer is wrong.
He will not remember it. The thought, the insight, the concept will
disappear. It may return, but you will not need it then,
or recall when it might have been appropriate.

Insights and perceptions pass through the mind like fleet fireflies.
Lit for an instant, then gone back into the dark. They are precious,
irreplaceable. Stop what you are writing and write them into a notebook,
onto a napkin, a scrap of paper. ANYWHERE. They are more important
than what you are writing now. What you are writing now is there.
It is visible, tangible. You will not lose the mood, the flow, the roll.
— **Leonard Bishop**

Either write something worth reading or do something worth writing.
— **Benjamin Franklin**

Topic 7: Public Relations Writing

Public Relations is about perceptions and reality, bringing them together or creating a clear distinction

The importance of good writing skills cannot be stressed enough when preparing for, or pursuing, a career in public relations. It's not that everyone in PR devotes all or even a great percentage of their time to writing – many in the practice don't – it is that writing is a very focused process and the basis of effective communication, and since that's also what PR is supposed to be, the connection is not much of a stretch. Expect the first question a prospective employer to ask someone applying for a PR job to be, "Can you write?"

Depending on the organization or makeup of the PR operation, the writer may or may not be part of the strategic planning of a project or campaign, but the work the writer generates will. That work will likely be in the form of:

- PR plans
- Press releases
- Pitch letters
- Backgrounders
- Fact sheets
- Bios
- Media alerts
- Speeches
- Talking points
- Mission statements
- Position papers
- White papers
- Blogs

- Web pages
- Advertorials
- VNRs
- Proposals

Whatever form or format the writer's efforts take, it is important to note that the image of public relations practitioners has taken a hit in recent years. Segments of the public view PR people as "spin doctors" whose function is to lie or misrepresent factual data in order to make unethical business or political interests appear in a more favorable light.

Unfortunately, some PR practitioners have been brought in to respond to several highly controversial issues and have done so with high-gloss, transparently insincere, contrived, and unconvincing campaigns. Public relations is not lying. Lying is lying and, unfortunately, the profession has been slow to protect and preserve its own image, while stretching credibility in the cause of some high-profile clients.

Writers who ignore or misrepresent facts that do not reflect favorably on their subjects face the same ethical problem as others in the employ of organizations in trouble and no evidence shows lying to be the solution.

Writers are obliged to adhere to ethical conduct, whether writing for newspapers, magazines, the electronic media, or for a PR firm.

There are three rules for writing.
Unfortunately, no one can agree what they are.
— **Somerset Maugham**

Writing the PR Plan

One of the most useful steps in the writing process is planning, yet it is often relegated to incidental status, if it's considered at all. In a perfect world, it might be fine to simply go on and act, respond or react as deemed necessary. But a public relations program is just that – a program – and, as such, it should be a series of coordinated acts geared to achieve specific goals. Writing the PR Plan creates the outline, checklist, or map to reach those goals.

A good model for the plan follows the form used in a larger marketing effort, of which PR and advertising are typically the central parts. The plan should begin with a:

- **Situation analysis** that describes the issue (or Issues) the plan will address;
- **Objectives** that spell out specifically what is to be accomplished;
- **Strategy** defining the approach that will be needed to reach the objectives;
- **Tactics** that list specific steps involved in executing the strategy;
- **Budget** detailing the costs of the tactics; and a
- **Timeline** indicating how long it is expected to take to execute the tactics that implement the strategy to reach the objectives and address the situation for the cost budgeted.

Though the previous sentence might suggest a variation on the "Twelve Days of Christmas," it is a simple, methodical process that leads to the development of a plan to create an organized effort in which the writer and others can do what needs to be done in a logical and orderly way.

Writing the Press Release

The press release is the essential tool of the public relations practitioner. Its purpose is to present information to members of the
media, such as editors, columnists, bloggers, and TV and radio
producers, to interest them in developing newspaper, magazine,
TV, radio, or online features about the company, product, organization, individual, or issue that is the subject of the release. It's a
pitch written in the format of a news story.

Note: A common question and point of some confusion and
debate is whether or not a "press release" and a "news release" are
the same instrument. Some teachers and practitioners consider
that to be the case. The author of this book, however, does not,
based on a belief that a news release must have "news" which,
by definition, has an element of timeliness. A press release has
information that may be timely or can be held for a future edition
or program a day, a week, a month, or a season later.

There is a fairly standard format for preparing press releases
going to print publications. The advent of the personal computer and the Internet has made some people feel as if new rules
now apply because everyone has access to a variety of fonts and
a rainbow of colors for typefaces. Press releases are information
vehicles, not artwork to hang on the refrigerator door. Editors
and producers expect to see certain protocols observed and if
the person sending the press release wants the information to be
used, it's a good idea to look buttoned-up and professional.

A press release should follow the same guidelines and journalistic principles of a news story, telling the reader *who, what,
where, when, why,* and *how* the information is relevant or presumably of interest to the reader. As it is an information vehicle for
the media, the press release should be objective and should not
be selling a company's product or an organization's message. It
should not include hyperbole or self-serving statements. If the
material is informative and well-written, some media do, in fact,

print, read, or use press release content exactly as it is provided to them.

The preferred format for press releases is the same as that of a manuscript prepared for presentation:

- Standard 8 ½" X 11" paper
- Margins of 1" to 1 ½" all around
- Double-spaced, using New Times Roman 12-point or Arial 11-point typeface font, which will produce…
- Approximately 250 words per page

The elements of the press release are:

- Contact information
- Embargo date or instructions for release of information
- Headline
- Dateline
- Lede (lead)
- Quotations
- Subject description, explanation/information
- Image statement
- Legal notice (as or if required)
- Sign-off

Contact information provides the people receiving the press release with the name, phone number, fax number, and e-mail address of someone to call for additional information about the content of the press release.

The **embargo date** or **instructions for release of information** lets the media know when it is okay to use the information – whether it is "for immediate release" or if it should be held until a specific date and/or time. This can be an issue if the information is about a company listed on a stock exchange, for example, and the information reaching the public before a certain time might create a sudden movement in the company's stock price.

Headline is now a common enough term that it can be assumed most people understand it is a short statement that informs the public what the information to follow is about. The headlines in press releases and news stories need not be complete sentences, but should contain at least a noun and a verb and be interesting and strong enough to make people want to read the story. The headline should not be simply a title. It should also not be suggestive of an ad or brochure headline that typically contains an element of hype or promotional language.

The **dateline** on a press release, as in a newspaper story, is below the headline (and the subhead if one is used) and precedes body copy. It consists of listing the city and date the information originates.

The **lede** (or **lead**) is the first sentences that introduce the subject of the release in a way that makes the reader want to read on. The term "burying the lede" means not getting into the most essential information about the subject until well into the story.

Quotations are not required in a press release, but usually enhance the content by including a relevant comment by someone involved in the story, such as a company CEO or an expert on the information presented. Such comments tend to fit best at the start of the second or third paragraph of the presentation.

The body copy of a press release is the **subject description, explanation/information** section and is typically a paragraph or two that follows the lede and a quote, and explains, elaborates, or more specifically identifies the subject, information, or participants in the story.

The **image statement** is a short paragraph describing the initiator of the press release (person, company, organization, or other entity) at the conclusion of the body of information, for purposes of identifying him, her, or it for readers who are unfamiliar with the initiator of the press release's history or background.

Legal notices (if required) might include "forward looking statements" or disclosures or disclaimers that may be required by law, regulation, or company policy as an accompaniment to all public documents and statements.

The **sign-off** is usually represented by the symbol #### at the bottom of the page at the very end of the press release. If the release is more than one page, the word "more" should appear at the bottom of each continuing page, with the following page clearly numbered to indicate its place in the continuation of the presentation.

The preferred length of a press release should be no more than two pages. If more information is necessary, offer it "on request" or as an attachment to the press release. Media people receive anywhere from dozens to hundreds of press releases each week and will be more favorably impressed by a succinct presentation of information pitched to them.

> *I keep six honest serving men*
> *They taught me all I knew;*
> *Their names are What and Why and When*
> *and How and Where and Who.*
> — **Rudyard Kipling**

> *Your stuff starts out being just for you... but then it goes out.*
> *Once you know what the story is and get it right – as right as you can,*
> *anyway – it belongs to anyone who wants to read it. Or criticize it.*
> — **Stephen King**

PRESS RELEASE

For information contact:
Joe Marconi
Marketing Communications, Inc.
708/588-9909
joemarconi@sbcglobal.net
for immediate release

New Book Recounts Memorable Days with Escaped Gorillas, Reluctant Elephants, Film Stars, and Pygmies

Dr. Fisher's Life on the Ark goes inside a big-city zoo, on jungle safaris,
and shares stories both silly and sad

(CHICAGO, December 17 –) Lester Fisher's touching, hilarious new book, Dr. Fisher's Life on the Ark (publisher, $26.95), recounts his life among the animals in a series of adventures, – all true and all delightful. From an alligator in the bathtub and his vet school escapades to organizing carrier pigeons for General Patton during World War II, the author faces the TV cameras, and gorillas in the mist. The book also includes a Forward by television and film actress Betty White.

Dr. Fisher first became the zoo doctor at Marlin Perkins's Lincoln Park Zoo and, ultimately, was named the zoo's director, holding that title for three decades. Immediately upon his taking charge in 1962, his series of colorful experiences and misadventures began. While caring for the world-famous lowland gorilla Bushman and a succession of prized great apes, Dr. Fisher embarked on collecting trips to Cameroon and numerous safari adventures to Africa, India, and around the world. He writes of encounters with Highlands warriors in Papua New Guinea, Pygmies of the Ituri Forest, and of black rhinos in Tanzania. Then it's back to the zoo for more animal antics and escapes in tales that are fun, poignant, entertaining, and occasionally scary.

Readers are also offered an inside look at some of the most memorable moments from Dr. Fisher's years on TV's The Ark in the Park and learn that taking animals on TV can be wildly funny and exciting, both on and off camera.

Pages later, the doctor is off to Sri Lanka to bring home a baby elephant, back for lunch with the founder of McDonald's, touring the Zoo with HRH Prince Philip of Great Britain, and playing host to diplomats, business leaders and movie stars. TV's Betty White has said Dr. Fisher's Life on the Ark offers many adventures, "some funny, some harrowing, but always interesting."

Racom Communications in Chicago is the publisher of *Dr. Fisher's Life on the Ark*. Books may be ordered online at www.racombooks.com.

####

Writing Pitch Letters

Just as the objective of a press release is to convince editors, columnists, and producers to generate feature stories on the subject of the release in the media, the pitch letter is another tool with the same ultimate goal. It is an alternative vehicle for attempting to get the attention of media people. A significant difference between the two is that, while 10 or 100 or 1,000 copies of a press release might be sent to a list of media, pitch letters are more singularly directed at particular editors or producers, mindful that publications and programs often have specific unique characteristics that the pitch should be tailored to exploit.

Pitch letters are exactly what the name implies – a proposed article or story idea pitched to members of the media.

The idea or strategy might be the brainchild of a PR account executive or a publicist, but the writer must frame it in a way that convinces an editor or producer it is both workable and good.

It's important to remember that, like most people, editors and producers do not appreciate having people tell them how to do their jobs, but they are receptive to ideas that make their jobs easier. A well-crafted pitch letter can offer editors and producers ideas for stories their audience will enjoy and benefit from reading or seeing.

A pitch letter is different from a press release in that it:

- is personalized to the editor, columnist or producer receiving it;
- is crafted to appeal to that person's particular type of audience;
- is brief, direct, uncomplicated, and straight to the point;
- may be timely and appropriate for the current schedule or editorial calendar;
- is not a transparently promotional or marketing-oriented piece;

197

- is newsworthy or otherwise has value to the media and audience;
- offers unbiased, recognized experts who can address the subject in an interesting, entertaining way.

The people receiving the pitch letters understand that the objective of the pitch is to have a story on the subject produced. The editor or producer wants and needs content for a publication or program so there is no need for either side to be either coy or overly aggressive or blatant in reviewing the pitch. When handled with subtlety, but with substance in content, everyone wins.

Consider the content of the press release shown in the example. A pitch letter to a specific editor or producer would offer to make available the author of the book described for an interview or a segment either at the media organization's offices or studio or onsite at a chosen location. the letter would indicate why and how the audience would benefit from such a piece being done with the author – how it would be entertaining and educational. Note that the offer of the author is for a limited time, which implies if the offer is not accepted it will be offered to a rival media company.

Why a pitch letter if a press release has already been issued? Not all press releases are used or even read. Most people, however, do read their mail and a letter pitching a story might well be more appealing than a more general announcement aimed at the media at-large.

The secret of good writing is to say an old thing in a new way or to say a new thing in an old way.
— **Richard Harding Davis**

The most original of authors are not so because they advance what is new, but more because they know how to say something, as if it had never been said before.
— **Johann Wolfgang Von Goethe**

Joe Marconi
Marketing Communications

June 26, 2006

Ms. Margaret Pergler,
Producer
The Today Show
30 Rockefeller Center
Room 568E-2
New York, NY 10112

Dear Ms. Pergler,

Dr. Les Fisher is on a first-name basis with an interesting group of gorillas, rhinos, alligators, and Pygmies and now he'd very much like to meet you. He's written a book called "Dr. Fisher's Life on the Ark" which recounts his experiences, including safari adventures to Africa and India, as well as encounters with Highlands warriors in Papua New Guinea, and much more. A very personable gentleman, he has original film footage, still photographs and a wealth of fascinating stories to share. We would be delighted to make Dr. Fisher available to viewers of The Today Show as part of our effort to introduce his book, a copy of which is enclosed.

I will contact you later this week to discuss what I believe would be an excellent booking for the show, a treat for your viewers, and a pleasure for Dr. Fisher.

Best regards,
Joe Marconi
Joe Marconi

Writing Backgrounders

A detailed book on the history of a company could be an excellent gift for shareholders, as well as a media tool or a PR device. A single page overview on the company is called a backgrounder and it is an important part of a press kit.

As the term implies, a backgrounder provides the media with background on a subject. In the case of a business organization or corporation, a backgrounder is simply a brief biography of a company, citing its history, its purpose, size, scope, key officers and significant participants, and highlights of its time in existence in a short, concise narrative.

This is not a commemorative anniversary book that recounts milestones or a timeline, laced with reminiscences, anecdotes, and self-congratulatory comments. The purpose of the backgrounder is to be used as a stand-alone document or as a component of a press kit, providing a short summary of relevant information to serve as a briefing for interviewers, reporters, and producers developing features on the subject.

A backgrounder, a fact sheet, and a brochure do (or can) essentially include the same information simply presented in different formats.

Writing a backgrounder follows the same principles as journalism, again addressing who, what, when, where, why, and how questions about the subject in a conversational, narrative form.

Most good writing is storytelling. A backgrounder is the story of its subject, told in the space of a page or two.

Have something to say, and say it as clearly as you can.
That is the only secret.
— **Matthew Arnold**

The Charles Financial Group
Company Background

The Company

The Charles Financial Group is a new kind of firm for financial institutions and other sophisticated traders. This New York Stock Exchange member organization was established in 2007 by a group of veteran industry professionals.

While Charles Financial Group provides a full range of services and a complete product offering – state-of-the art technology, open architecture to accommodate various trading platforms, a precision back office, and a solid trading floor operation that includes the most experienced brokers and traders on any major exchange – it is the customer that defines the terms of the relationship.

The Market

Sophisticated traders with an understanding of the market and its uses know that for more than a century, a variety of investment instruments have been used to manage risk while exploring a wide range of opportunities. Charles Financial Group is unique. It is sensitive to the rhythm of the market – to its tempo – and to maintaining a sense of balance.

No one can predict the direction of the market. Sophisticated traders outperform other traders because they know the market and have the resources to follow through on their decisions.

Technology, the introduction of new products, and the expansion of global markets have created new opportunities for sophisticated traders – and heightened the need for a strong organization with a solid understanding of the markets. That's The Charles Financial Group.

The Mission

Charles Financial Group's mission is to deliver creative solutions through an individualized approach, accommodating the demands of even the largest financial institutions with superior order execution and clearing services at competitive prices.

Like the old line about the weather – everybody talks about it, but no one ever actually does anything about it – everyone in business promises service, but few ever actually deliver on those promises. Charles Financial Group is built on a promise to deliver an extraordinary level of service. The firm's management is committed to delivering the quality service they would demand for themselves.

Customers choose the services they need and want, from traditional order execution only and clearing services to full facilities management.

The People

Charles Financial Group management team and brokers, traders and professional staff – separately and together – bring an unparalleled level of knowledge of the market, trading experience, operational expertise and skill to providing customers with uniquely tailored services developed according to customer specifications.

Charles Financial Group executives each have more than two decades of financial services industry experience, much of it acquired while holding senior level positions at some of the leading firms in the business.

201

Writing Fact Sheets

As noted in the preceding example and below, the corporate back-grounder and fact sheet contain the same basic information. It is the format that is different, a function of the company's personal choice, as well as, in a public relations sense, the type of image it wants to present – somewhat more formal (the backgrounder's narrative presentation) or a more informal, brief, crisp presentation (the fact sheet's bullet points) that can be read virtually at a glance.

Some instructors prefer a fact sheet format that literally lists the words who, what, when, where, and why in a left-hand column, followed by the details of those point to their right. Many instructors in writing classes – this one included – believe that format resembles an announcement or invitation more than it does a fact sheet and favor the simple bullet-point list as shown.

The Charles Financial Group
Fact Sheet

- established in 2007
- founded by a group of veteran financial industry professionals
- senior partners each have more than two decades of financial services industry experience
- offers an experienced team of brokers, traders, and professional staff
- provides a full range of financial services and products
- is a member of the New York Stock Exchange
- offers state-of-the art technology, open architecture to accommodate various trading platforms
- provides a precision back office operating team
- has a solid trading floor operation that includes the industry's most experienced brokers and traders
- guarantees tailored services developed according to customer specifications

For more information contact The Charles Financial Group, Chicago

---

Writing Bios

Who are the people who make things happen? How do they do it? What makes them in any way different from the mail carrier, ice cream vendor, or anyone else? And if they are just like everyone else, how is it they have been identified as the ones who make things happen?

People want to know. But in the event people don't want to know, the writer's job is to make the subject somehow appear more interesting than the "everyman" character who appears in silhouette in ads.

How does someone make a person seem interesting to strangers when that person may or may not be all that exciting. It's similar to the challenge in writing a résumé when one doesn't think he or she has actually done all that much. The basic writer's answer: get it down on paper – no matter how uninteresting it seems – and edit in or out what's the most descriptive, colorful, or noteworthy information. Fill the page with associations or memories of:

- schools
- clubs
- fraternities
- civic groups
- awards or honors
- hobbies
- volunteer work
- advice received from a parent
- a character who was an inspiration in childhood
- a story or book that influenced the subject or seem to reflect what he or she thought or dreamed…

As the backgrounder is the history or "life story" of a product, company, or organization, the bio – short for biography – is the

story of or about a person who is part of the company or organization and has been singled out as a spokesperson or VIP worth
knowing about. Unlike the standard life story biography, corporate executives' bios do not begin with the birth of the individual
or focus on his or her family life or childhood. They tell the story
in terms of highlights of the individual's career and his or her
relationship and contribution to the entity that is the subject of
the public relations effort. It is, in effect, a résumé presented in
narrative form in as few words as possible.

THE CHARLES FINANCIAL GROUP
Richard Alan Charles, CEO

Rick Charles is perhaps best known within the financial services industry throughout the world for his 19 years with the BankUSA organization, the last seven as its president. After retiring in 2000, he returned
two years later to serve as Vice-Chairman. His considerable experience
has included executive management, head of brokerage operations and
business interests in the United States, Europe, and Asia, where he specialized in risk management and portfolio oversight activities.

He established successful branch operations in London and Hong Kong
and was responsible for overseeing Chicago and New York operations,
institutional sales and marketing, risk management, foreign exchange,
and correspondent broker relationships. He has chaired key industry
committees on management, technology, finance, law, and compliance.

A much sought-after speaker at major industry conferences around the
world, most notably in the United States, the U.K., Germany, France,
Japan, China, and Turkey, he has also contributed articles to major industry publications and the *International Herald Tribune*.

A graduate of the University of Chicago, Rick now again makes the city
his home.

Writing Media Alerts

What's a media alert? Ask different communicators or PR people and you will get a few different answers. To many, a "media alert" is the same as a press release. Others use the term synonymously with media advisory, though what is delivered under that title seems little more than an announcement resembling a party invitation that literally lists the words who, what, where, and when vertically, followed by the expected name, location, event title, and date. It would seem there is not much there to justify an "alert" or an "advisory." Usually the words "alert" or "advisory" are followed by some urgent news announcement or emergency warning.

The Ohio Arts Council has a good take on the subject:

A media alert is intended for more urgent matters. If there is an approaching deadline, such as an event canceled abruptly or scheduled to occur in three days, an alert would be the most appropriate communications tool. Media alerts should be used sparingly and only when something happens that cannot be controlled. They should not be a substitute for lack of planning.

Guidelines for media alerts:

- Keep them short and simple and direct. Unlike a press release, the media alert is not the vehicle to tell a story.

- Don't include quotes, promotional taglines, or other non-essential information.

- Clearly identify the most important point and indicate why it is newsworthy or what qualifies it as requiring an "alert" designation.

- Label the alert appropriately in large, bold type to distinguish it from normal press releases directed to the media.

- Use media alerts sparingly.

Too frequent use of media alerts can create an unfavorable impression with the press.

Speechwriting

Whose voice is it anyway? And what is it saying?

Speechwriting is an oddly unknowable mixture of presentation and content. Some great speeches are cheered, but when studied later found to not have much to say. That is a case of an especially good speaker demonstrating power in the presentation. Other speeches may have been quietly delivered to small audiences, but when read later proved to be so meaningful, insightful, and powerful as to be quoted and called "great" decades or centuries later.

The speechwriter's role is an interesting one. People think of presidential speechwriters and wonder why the job is even necessary. Shouldn't, after all, a leader know what he or she stands for and wants to say or propose and just be able to get up and say it? Isn't the speechwriter playing a role in creating policy or exercising powers or influence that no one elected a speechwriter to have?

The answers are "yes" and "maybe."

What the speechwriter is supposed to be doing is not formulating policy or beliefs, but organizing and assisting in presenting information conveyed to him or her so that it might be delivered in a clear, concise, and unambiguous way that will resonate and not be misunderstood. Obviously, it doesn't always turn out that way. The aim is that a lot of potentially important information can be presented so it not only makes sense, but is persuasive and generates agreement and support.

The writer's approach to speechwriting must consider whether the writer will be the person delivering the speech or if it will be written to be delivered by someone else. It's an obvious and important distinction. The latter being about getting the content developed in the speaker's own "voice" – a cadence and style – and not using terms the reader or listener does not accept as reflective of the speaker's personality, manner, or beliefs.

While it might seem like a simplistic point, writing words to be spoken is quite different from writing words to be read. One major difference is sentences. Writers are taught to write in complete sentences. That works best on the printed page. However, most people don't speak in complete sentences, speaking normally instead of in phrases – fragments – often lacking nouns or verbs, engaging in rhetoric, and using expressions that carry power when delivered verbally, but are flat and largely emotionless on a page. Consider:

What!

A joke, right?

Huh?

Well... okay, then

That's something else...

Hey, different strokes...

No, really...

Comedians usually have a device – a phrase uttered quickly after a punch line ("but I wanna tell ya...") – to serve as a segue or transition between jokes or sections of a speech, delivered during an audience response (laughter or applause). In a written version, to be read silently, these blurbs only work in quotes, parentheses, or asides. But in a spoken presentation, dropping such phrases or fragments can make a speaker seem more engaging, confident, or relaxed.

A speech is a scripted monologue, ideally memorized and recited from memory, as if spoken extemporaneously.

In reality, many if not most people read all or much of their speeches from written pages placed before them at a lectern. Speakers on television often rely on off-screen teleprompters or cue-cards to provide a copy of the speech to read, while appearing to be speaking directly to the audience.

How important is it to not read a speech?

Teachers and coaches in public speaking stress that delivering a speech without a script or notes makes for a vastly more effective presentation, comparing it to a performance by an actor. Who, after all, wants to see actors reading their lines from scripts instead of seeming to be delivering them extemporaneously, naturally, or dramatically in performance?

An excellent point, except that in most cases public speakers are not actors, they are public officials, corporate spokespersons, the chairperson of the Program Committee, or someone offering information that, in both content and context, should not be regarded as a performance.

The speaker, to be effective, should appear to know the subject material contained in the speech very well. If the speaker is regarded as knowledgeable and credible on a subject, having a written document to refer to is a small issue.

If, however, the speaker is not viewed as credible or is unknown to the audience and appears to need a written speech to address a subject about which he or she is supposed to be well-informed, the issue is not one of reading or not reading, it's a matter of credibility.

If the speaker is delivering a speech as part of a public relations effort, the apparent knowledge and credibility of the speaker is the very essence of the presentation and, perhaps, of the campaign. For this reason, the speaker must appear to really know what he or she is talking about.

The biggest reason speeches fall flat is not because speakers read or don't read the words, it's because the speakers are poorly prepared or appear to be seeing (and reading) the words for the first time and do not seem to believe what they are saying enough to sell the message.

It's not about selling the speech – it's about selling the speaker.

The speech should be a speaker having a conversation with the audience, making points he or she believes, and being persuasive in presenting those points.

From the speechwriter's perspective, let's focus here on the content, but first, let's dispense with a few myths about speeches and speechwriting:

1. A speech must include an opening (icebreaker) joke and have at least another joke or two in the body of text.

2. A speech must include quotes from St. Augustine, Benjamin Franklin, Mark Twain, Abraham Lincoln, John F. Kennedy, and/or Woody Allen. Hopefully, all of them.

3. A speech must be accompanied by a PowerPoint presentation. (Canadian definition of an expert – "Someone from the States with a PowerPoint.")

None of these are true, but you wouldn't know it from most speeches. It's a fine line – a lot of audiences are turned off by the predictable references, yet still enjoy something comfortable and familiar. The solution is to give them something interesting, informative and entertaining, though not an overworked gag or reference to the current celebrity in the news. Unless the speaker is a comedian, don't try to turn the occasion of giving a speech into a late-night monologue.

- A speaker's opening is similar to a guest arriving: a friendly greeting, an expression of appreciation for being invited, some impromptu light banter about others in attendance, acknowledgement of the host and any previous speakers.

- A speech, as with any other piece of writing, should emphasize content – give audience members something they didn't know or, at least, something they didn't know is the opinion of the speaker and put an interesting twist on it using words and phrases that sound as if they would actually come from the speaker.

- The standard rules apply: content should be fact-checked, specific, and presented in a logical way that the audience can absorb.

- The speech should be presented in the speaker's style, whether the speaker is the writer or someone else. Don't use obscure references, inside jokes, jargon, foreign terms, or expressions the speaker wouldn't use or the audience wouldn't understand or appreciate.

- The speech should reflect what the speaker thinks, feels, believes, represents, and knows.

- The speech should be written out, using short sentences with pauses at regular intervals indicating where the speaker should take a breath or wait for a reaction or for the words to resonate – to hang in the air for a few seconds or to sink in.

- Quotes from experts who either support or challenge the speaker's comments can make a presentation more interesting or authoritative.

- Statistics (numbers, dollars, percentages) interest audiences and often cause people to react. Whether the numbers are high or low, they can make a speech more interesting or informative.

- Whether the speech is read or recited, the speaker should read it through several times – aloud – before delivering it to be certain the words and phrases flow easily, "sound right," and "work" comfortably within the speaker's normal breath range, pronunciation, and vocal style.

Research shows that speaking in public is most people's greatest fear. With the right words, rehearsed and well presented, that doesn't need to be the case.

Talking Points

A talking point has, along with spin doctor, become a popular term that media people associate with public relations and usually in negative terms. Talking points are ideas, carefully thought-through and prepared in advance, made available to members of a team or organization, speakers, spokespersons, and others interested in a particular subject to guide or keep a discussion on track and maintain consistency with either the policy of an organization or an individual or organization's earlier positions.

In terms of content, talking points may or may not be factual. Sometimes they could simply be interpretations or, for argument's sake, opposing points-of-view to stimulate conversation, debate, or further study.

Political organizations particularly use talking points in strategies that challenge or undermine the positions of their opponents.

The term talking point, like propaganda, has a negative connotation to some people, as if it is information without foundation or credibility. That's not the case. Talking points are a list of comments that help make a persuasive argument for or against a subject. It is only when the talking points are repeated too often by too many spokespersons that the weight of the argument seems to diminish as the case becomes overdone, repetitious, tiresome, and appears too organized or rehearsed, causing them to become progressively less persuasive.

Think tanks, which are typically positioned as research organizations, but are in many instances public relations units, are credited with developing talking points, which are then offered and presented as if they are bite-size versions of "position papers" – arguments laid out as a lawyer might prepare a case in order to win both a judgment and public opinion. Unfortunately too many of the talking points are crafted not for content, but to be repeated endlessly, sounding like advertising jingles or bumper sticker phrases – biting, sarcastic, insulting, often silly in their al-literation, and undermining their ability to be taken seriously.

As with much about public relations today, talking points have gotten a bum rap, largely because of practitioners who lack a basic respect for the audience's intelligence and a lack of real knowledge of their subjects. Making strong, persuasive, serious arguments will go a long way to undoing the damage.

For the writer of talking points, the drill by now should be familiar:

- know the audience and its level of knowledge, sophistication, and tolerance
- brainstorm the possibilities
- be credible
- don't offend
- check facts
- use short sentences
- avoid "cuteness" or being too glib
- don't overuse words and phrases
- make a persuasive argument
- keep it simple
- write in language at a level the audience understands

Remember the case is best served by winning agreement, not by having everyone echoing or parroting the same, tired phrases.

Mission Statements

A mission statement, like a marketing plan, takes different forms, serves different purposes, and is imbued with different perceptions of value and importance. There are also differing opinions about exactly what is, and if or why, it's necessary to have a mission statement.

One definition holds that "the mission statement is a crucial element in the strategic planning of a business organization and can be a building block for an overall strategy and development of more specific functional strategies."

Another, considerably less wordy take on it, says that "a mission statement is a brief description of a company or organization's purpose."

Still another attempt at definition puts it this way: "A mission statement answers the question, 'Why do we exist?'"

Just as some marketing plans are long and focus on minutiae, micromanaging, and emphasizing accountability rather than marketing, others are more of a short "to-do" list, similarly corporate mission statements can be long-winded, rambling, self-serving and, for the most-part unread and unheeded, or they can be a sentence or two and make a direct point.

If the question goes to why a company exists, most people agree there is no more direct or honest answer than "to make money."

Obviously that is not the case for the not-for-profit or non-profit corporations. Still, on the "for-profit" side, many people question the actual need for a mission statement. Without questioning the nobility or otherwise lofty pretensions of some corporate executives, the simple value of mission statements is in their having a public relations purpose. Telling specific segments of the public what a company or organization stands for can be the reason it finds acceptability or support and a constituency... or not.

The statement should ideally come before a business plan is written so that "mission" can be reflected in the presentation of what the company will do and how it will do it. Putting the overall idea into a couple of sentences can create an underlying theme that is represented throughout.

Keep it simple. Some example of corporate mission statements:

Provide society with superior products and services by developing innovations and solutions that improve the quality of life and satisfy customer needs, and to provide employees with meaningful work and advancement opportunities, and investors with a superior rate of return. (Merck Pharmaceutical)

A computer on every desktop and in every home, running Microsoft software (Microsoft)

Organize the world's information and make it universally accessible and useful. (Google)

Simply put, in as few words as possible, the mission statement should tell why the company exists and what it's going to do.

*First, I do not sit down at my desk to put into verse something
that is already clear in my mind. If it were clear in my mind,
I should have no incentive or need to write about it.
We do not write in order to be understood,
we write in order to understand.*
— **Robert Cecil Day-Lewis**

*Endless conflicts. Endless misunderstanding. All life is that.
Great and little cannot understand one another.*
— **H.G. Wells**

Position Papers

People grow up hearing the term position paper, but what is it exactly? Like so much else, over time its meaning has been modified a bit.

A position paper is a critical examination of texts by one or more authors. In short, it's a written opinion on something. It takes sides on an issue. That's the definition. But in public relations terms, the importance of having a written document called a position paper to point to (and quote from) is that the designation itself has a ring of authority. Never mind that it might be a written opinion prepared by the very person presenting it as an authoritative document; it carries the ring of authority and, in PR, perception is (sometimes) reality.

The position paper is not a study, which should include objective data that has been collected and analyzed against what is known and not known to produce a reasoned conclusion. A position paper, typically prepared to reflect the attitudes and policies of public officials, government agencies, institutions, or candidates for office, is today a document clarifying a position, offered as an official statement, for the record.

A writer planning to write a position paper needs to:

- organize and outline facts relating to an opinion or viewpoint on the subject of the paper;
- indicate what the position is as a foundation to build a case for resolution of differing points-of-view on the subject;
- present a unique, if biased, solution or approach to solving a problem;
- frame the discussion in order to define the "playing field" and provide an advantageous position in comparison to those of opponents and/or competitors;
- preface the document with a page establishing the writer's credibility to define and demonstrate a command of the issues and research;

215

- present a forceful argument;
- be consistent in maintaining a position.

The format of the paper should be adhere to guidelines determined by its sponsor, committee, or the entity behind the creation of the document, or in a form that is the usual and customary presentation for such a paper.

Include the topic, date, title, purpose, and identify the author on a title page and…

- Know the audience for the document.
- Write a topic sentence or two that attracts attention and summarizes the issue.
- Inform the reader of the point of view of the paper.
- If the paper represents a group, organization, or a committee, do not write in the first person.
- Aim for a document of two to five pages, following a fairly standard format established by early successful position papers.
- Develop supporting evidence for both sides, including factual knowledge, statistical evidence, and authoritative testimony.
- Identify issues and biases, keeping in mind the audience that will receive or read the paper.
- Assume familiarity with basic concepts, but define unfamiliar terms or concepts and provide meanings that define points of departure.
- Invite others who support or agree with the position to assist in developing an argument.
- Become familiar with those who disagree, anticipate their criticism, and prepare a defense.
- Summarize their argument and evidence, then refute it in the document.

Focus on one to three main points to develop and have each point include:

- a general statement of the position
- an elaboration that references documents and source data
- past experiences and authoritative testimony
- conclusion restating the position

Establish flow from paragraph to paragraph.

- Write in a confident, active voice.
- Quote sources to establish authority and reinforce credibility.
- Stay focused on the point-of-view throughout the document.
- Use logical arguments.
- Don't lapse into summary in the development – wait for the conclusion.

The conclusion of the Position Paper should:

- Summarize, then conclude the argument.
- Refer to the first paragraph or opening statements, as well as to the main points to be sure the conclusion restates the main ideas and reflects the importance of the argument, and concludes logically.

Revise, proofread, and build a strong case to achieve the desired objective. Like much of writing, what essentially changes is the format. That is, a position paper is similar in many respects to a persuasive essay, an advertorial, or a proposal. It's simply another document to help make a case.

A Good Position Paper should…

- be in the author's own words
- have a clear purpose
- be well organized
- flow smoothly

- be clear
- be complete
- be focused
- be substantive
- be correct
- be mechanically proper in its presentation form, adhering to rules of style and usage
- be creative
- raise new questions
- answer old questions in new ways
- see new things
- see old things in new ways
- make an original point.

If written well, a position paper can be cited as the definitive, authoritative document on a subject, despite the fact that it is essentially a statement of opinion.

*Write it, even if you think it's terrible. Don't prevent yourself
from jotting down a word, phrase, or paragraph just because
it "isn't quite right" or "it won't work." Maybe it will, maybe it
won't, but it's better to write it down, you can always edit later.
And you don't want to stop yourself before you even get started!
The point isn't to use everything you write. You can't be expected
to pop out perfect prose your first time out!
Write now, edit later.*

— **Cristine Grace**

Writing crystallizes thought and thought produces action.

— **Paul J. Meyer**

Writing for the Web and Blogs

It seems almost obligatory that everything written about writing for the Web begin with the words, *People read differently from screens so writers must write differently for them than for the printed paper page.*

With the requirement to include that obvious point satisfied, it may also be noted that entire books are written about writing for the Web. Good writing, however, is good writing and once the principles are understood and why "breaking the rules" is more acceptable in some situations, but not others, the venue where the writer's good words appear – a book, newspaper, a magazine, script, ad, a proposal or plan, or a Web site – become a matter of adaptability to conditions, not about having to learn a different way to write.

As with much on this subject, some will disagree. Ad people view their type of writing as a specific art form and certainly poets don't want to be told they have much in common with people who write catalogs and package labels. A certain romance is sacrificed once that theory is validated. Many Web writers also view themselves as a breed apart from other writers, their platform being the centerpiece of the most significant development since the printing press.

Maybe.

But when the writing is for public relations purposes, the "anything goes" approach must be reigned in to accomplish the objective.

The term blog is short for Weblog or Web Log, which is defined as frequently updated Web sites containing dated entries arranged in reverse chronological order so the most recent post appears first.

The "posts" – the updated entries on blogs – are listed sequentially, from the most recent to all that preceded it, and readers can track the continuity of the entire written presentation or go to specific dates or months they want to read. Some blogs are set up to allow the writers to categorize specific blog posts, meaning they can define categories they tend to write about, such as news, sports, politics, religion, or other interests. Later, when they write a new post that relates to a category, they place that post in the category. By linking content to categories, readers can skim through past blogs, filtering their reading by viewing only the posts in categories that interest them.

Over the years, writers have experimented with the genre and developers have created new software to publish and archive blogs. Blogging has evolved to include photoblogs, which typically include photographs with commentary; videoblogs that synthesize video with commentary; fiction blogs, where writers can post short stories or continuing-series fiction; and mo'blogging (mobile blogging), with pictures, video and text posted from a camera phone directed instantly to the Web.

A writer who chooses to create and continue posting to a blog can explore opportunities, build a portfolio of work, and perhaps, through this method of modern self-publishing, find an appreciative audience.

Today, many high-profile leading writers in their fields, such as Dave Barry and Andrew Sullivan, who have enjoyed success with their books and newspaper or magazine columns, have found additional loyal readers and fans through their blogs. It is also a good outlet for a writer to explore other areas of writing – other genres, from politics to humor to poetry.

For many writers this is a preferred alternative to traditional publishing as it affords an uncommon degree of independence. Some people have referred to the Internet and blogs as the first (or last) truly free press. That's an interesting perspective, but it's worth noting that such freedom has also brought grief. A great deal of Internet writing and blogging has resulted in a incorrect or intentionally misleading information due to an absence of oversight and mandatory fact-checking, as exists with newspapers and magazines.

On the positive side, a blog can:

- encourage daily writing, which can stimulate creativity and productivity;
- help improve writing skills;
- provide a place to share reflections and insights;
- create a dialogue with other writers and readers;
- allow experimenting with a new genre of communication.

In the opinion of writers who've explored the venue, blogs get mixed reviews. Blogs tend to bury past entries in archives, emphasizing the present. Blogging isn't the best rhetoric for sustained discourse, but blogs are useful for providing daily insights, brief abstracts, and annotations. Most blogs are brief, though some are extensive. Most blogs are also monological, meaning they reflect one person's thoughts and emotions. For a new writer wanting to experiment and get feedback, there are worse ways to go.

In many respects the Internet is still a relatively young platform for writers in that it is still very much evolving. At the same time, the Internet is the medium of choice for a generation, both in terms of personal communication and collecting information. As such, for writers, Internet writing – and blogging – is both the future and the order of the day. When all the dust settles, it should be expected that good writing will still be good writing, but, as has happened so often before, the parchment/scroll/writing pad/copy paper/notebook screen has changed.

If you can't annoy somebody, there is little point in writing.
— **Kingsley Amis**

Advertorials

An advertorial is an ad written to mirror the look and tone of a newspaper editorial. Historically, editorials have presented the opinions and recommendations of an editor, an editorial board or a publisher. Editorials are not objective, but are presumed to be based on serious research, deliberation, and consideration. As such, they care an assumed weight of value, importance, and authority. The term "advertorial" comes from combining "advertisement" and "editorial" – a portmanteau (see the lexicon at the back section of the book).

Advertorials differ from press releases, which are sent to publications in the hope of generating a story. A person or an organization running an advertorial must pay the media company both for carrying the material presented, as it would in the placement of any other ad, and an additional "premium" for positioning the advertorial near the publication's traditional editorial page or section. The idea is to convey to readers that the advertorial represents a position or view of the advertiser in the same way an editorial reflects the view of a publication.

Press releases that result in stories in the media are placed without payment to the media company, but the originator of the press release also has no control over the copy content or whether or where in the publication a story might appear. A final story created in response to a press release might even reference competitors more prominently or favorably.

Most reputable publications will not accept advertisements that look exactly like stories or features in the newspapers or magazines in which they are appearing. The differences may be subtle, and disclaimers, such as the word "advertisement" in small type might be enough to satisfy some media policies.

Sometimes euphemisms describing the advertorial as a "special promotional feature" or "special section" of "sponsored report" are used.

Advertorials commonly promote new types of technology or medical treatments, such as a new form of surgical procedure. The tone is closer to that of a press release or brochure copy than of an objective news story.

Advertorials can also be printed as entire newspaper sections, inserted the way fliers or sale material is to a paper.

But most commonly, advertorials are used by organizations under fire to explain their side of the story and rebut attacks or criticism.

Mobil Oil has long been a major proponent of advertorials as part of its efforts to get its version of events in the energy industry into the American press when it believed it was not being treated fairly in general media coverage. The political and media advisor Fred Dutton developed a strategy to publish Mobil Oil's opinion as a paid advertisement on editorial pages of major newspapers across the country. The strategy was successful in getting the company's message out to the public, as well as to politicians who invariably read newspaper editorial pages, believing they are a reflection of public opinion. Mobil Oil quickly became identified with this unique advertising strategy, which it continues to follow in its current incarnation as Exxon/Mobil Oil. Microsoft is another large organization that uses advertorials to present its side of the story on often controversial issues.

Except for its formatting – to visually suggest the traditional newspaper editorial – the advertorial is, in terms of content, quite similar to the concept of writing "An open letter to our customers (or shareholders or employees)."

For the writer, writing an advertorial is a PR assignment, much like writing a press release which, at its best, reads as though it were written by a journalist.

VNRs
Video News Releases: Pictures Do the Talking

A video news release (VNR) is a short video segment created by a public relations firm, advertising agency, marketing firm, corporation, public service group, special interest group, or government agency and provided without charge to television stations for the purpose of informing the public, shaping public opinion, or promoting and publicizing individuals, products, services, issues, causes, or virtually any other subject. VNRs are basically video versions of press releases with the provider hoping to secure a TV feature placement, while having control of the content.

News reports may incorporate a VNR in whole or part if the news producer feels it contains information appropriate to a story or of interest to viewers.

Critics of VNRs have called the practice deceptive and a propaganda technique – attaching a negative connotation to the term.

The basis of much of the criticism is that, in most cases, the segment is not identified to the viewers as having been provided by someone with a vested interest or a point of view regarding the story. For the writer, the task is basically writing a TV feature, in effect adapting a traditional press release to a narrative script format. It is the PR entity providing it that must deal with the ethical issues VNRs may present.

In a thousand words I can have the Lord's Prayer,
the 23rd Psalm, the Hippocratic Oath, a sonnet by Shakespeare,
the Preamble to the Constitution, Lincoln's Gettysburg Address
and almost all of the Boy Scout Oath.
Now exactly what picture were you planning to trade for all that?
— **Roy H. Williams**

Proposals

Writing proposals is an area covered elsewhere in this book, but is worth noting here because it is does have some bearing on public relations writing. When a proposal is submitted, whether it is a pitch for a new account at an advertising or PR agency or to win approval for an idea or project, it is a form of public relations, in that it creates, exploits, or attempts to change an opinion and its objective is to persuade the reader of the proposal to accept or agree to a particular project or program being presented.

Briefly, the formula for constructing a proposal is the same as that of a planning document. If the proposal is adopted, it then becomes the plan – the working outline for the program. Accordingly, include a brief situation analysis, statement of objectives, strategy outline, examples of tactics, a proposed budget, and timeline.

A proposal may well be the first document or contact someone has with its originating entity (agency or firm). The writer should:

- Begin with an index or table of contents.
- Make the document easy to read.
- Write clear headings.
- Keep paragraphs short.
- Number the pages.
- Check and re-check for mistakes in both the content and typographical errors.
- Specific information should be the centerpiece of the proposal, such as ideas or recommendations.
- Invite inquiries relating to the proposal content.
- Always accompany the proposal with a short cover letter.

For a writer, helpful advice about remembering to number pages and check for mistakes has got to seem bush league. Alas, it's usually some small glitch, like a typo, a misspelled or omitted word that gets attention of a negative sort. The writer is expected to write the proposal well and the heartbreaker is always the good proposal that gets kicked out because it failed to arrive on time or was found to have too many typos, reflecting badly on its writer and sender.

*People are always blaming their circumstances for what they are.
I don't believe in circumstances. The people who get on in this world are
the people who get up and look for the circumstances they want,
and, if they can't find them, make them.*
— **George Bernard Shaw**

I admire anybody who has the guts to write anything at all.
— **E. B. White**

*The most valuable of all talents is that of
never using two words when one will do.*
— **Thomas Jefferson**

Topic 8: Advertising Writing

As with other sections of this book, many volumes have been produced specifically about writing ads. Advertising is one of the rare subjects where pharmacist and coal miner alike can agree. They may not be experts, but they know what they like. In a way, they are experts.

Everyone has an opinion about advertising, particularly television advertising. And the print ads that catch the reader's eye usually manage to do so because a photograph or a headline makes the reader pause, smile, gasp, or experience outrage. Without question, the headline is the most important part of the ad where the writer is involved. If the reader is not drawn to the headline, he or she will not likely read the copy that follows.

If a writer ever wanted a chance to be creative, the headline is that chance – particularly in advertising.

Many ad copywriters love the business and the process and become truly great at mastering its principles and making a mark on business that can be felt for generations. Others use advertising as a stepping-stone to careers in film, television, other forms of writing, or entrepreneurial endeavors that require creativity, style, imagination, and an ability to persuade – to use words in a way that makes people want to react, often with great enthusiasm.

It starts with a headline… then, it's about the words.

What makes great ad copy? Great minds differ. People have a lot of theories, and here's one that makes as much sense as the others: In Thomas Berger's *Little Big Man*, the old Indian, looking at the sky after he'd finished his rain dance, says, "Sometimes the magic works, and sometimes it doesn't."

That's a lot like advertising.

Fortunately, to get down the basics of writing good advertising copy, the record of what works and what doesn't is a little better than it is for rain dancing, though perhaps not much.

One veteran copywriter put it this way: "What makes it difficult for the uninitiated is that what you may judge to be great copy because of the sheer poetry, imagery, sound, and lyricism, may be lousy for accomplishing the mission of the ad."

As advertising veteran Ron Cohn noted, "It's difficult to meet expectations when you don't know what those expectations are."

Writing good advertising copy must begin by defining the objectives of the ad campaign, as well as of the specific ad. They determine and influence the copy and keep the copywriter focused. The copy platform is a clear statement of the copy objectives, focus, and approach. It should guide the writing to achieve the objective of the ad.

AIDA

Veteran copywriter Robert W. Bly describes "the motivating sequence" for writing ads and PR material as "AIDA" creating **A**ttention, **I**nterest, turning that into **D**esire and, finally, initiating **A**ction.

Get the reader's or the viewer's attention with a headline or an illustration or a photograph or a creative layout – something that attracts or disrupts the routine and draws the eye or ear, grabs attention, creates interest, arouses desire, and invites or prompts action. The ad copy expands and sustains the interest generated by the headline

Of course it's easier to tell someone to do it than to actually do it. Writing ad copy involves a different kind of creativity than other types of writing. Good creative writing, while it should stir feelings and generate a response, doesn't necessarily have to excite or motivate a reader to act. Ad copy does.

Fortunately the advertising business is one that has its Hall of Fame to turn to – the words of David Ogilvy, Leo Burnett, Bill Birnbach, Howard Gossage, and dozens of others. Read them, take their advice, let them explain what works, what doesn't work, and why.

Most great ad writers say to get inside the heads of consumers, a writer must know what they like, what they want, what makes them happy, what makes them cry. Write for their needs and wants and dreams. Give them "permission to believe" and ask for a "willing suspension of disbelief" for them to accept for a moment that a car can fly, a horse can sing, and a new breath mint will make them more attractive or sexy or cause the sun to shine on a rainy day.

The ad copywriter's creativity is drawn from imagination and fantasy, from asking what if...?

The limits of copywriting are imposed by the medium, not the writer's mind. The reality of the fantasy is that only so much cleverness, wisdom, information, and promises of value will fit into a 10, 20 or 30-second TV or radio spot, or three-inch/one-column ad, or on a billboard atop a building, viewed from a car passing it at 65 miles per hour. Ad writing is one of the few disciplined, focus areas of writing that allows a writer almost free reign on coming up with ideas for how what needs to be conveyed can be conveyed.

Here's the drill:

- Know the audience for the ad.
- Respect the consumer.
- Believe what you are writing.
- Promise a benefit.
- Be credible... except for the singing horse, dancing cat, and flying car.
- Be persuasive.

- Be interesting.
- Create desire.
- Motivate action – Don't just write or say "call today" or "act now" – make an offer of something cool or free from your knowledge of what they want.
- Write short sentences and phrases.
- Use easy and familiar words and terms.
- Be concise.
- Be natural – to be persuasive does not require formality.
- Stay in the present – write in present tense.
- Use an active (but not an over-the-top) voice.
- Avoid overused words and phrases (see the clichés in the lexicon section).
- Don't trash the competition – stay focused on the message.
- Be honest and ethical.

And some tips from *The Copy Workshop Workbook*:

- Develop a short, straightforward writing style.
- Build a working vocabulary for the subject of the ad – nouns, verbs, adjectives, slang, jargon, interesting ideas, facts and figures, figures of speech.
- Talk person to person – talk to people, not at them.
- Remember the most important person is not the writer, but the person hearing or reading the writer's words.
- Find your verb – your job is to move people; activate your writing.
- Challenge yourself.

One final point: few people laugh as loudly or enjoy themselves as much as ad copywriters exploring ways to make something happen. Sometimes the magic works.

Topic 9: Writing the Press Kit

The press kit or media kit or media packet is a very buttoned-up term for a pocket folder containing material assembled for presentation to the media for use in developing a feature on a particular subject. The same packets are often used for sales presentations or at trade shows or security analyst meetings, and certainly at press briefings.

The purpose of the packet is to provide enough information to create a clear understanding of the subject, presenting lists of contacts, samples of products, ad slicks, templates, transcripts of interviews or speeches, copies of earlier feature articles, literature – whatever it takes to help the recipient – particularly a reporter, editor, or TV or radio producer – get the story right.

The usual elements of the press kit are:

- one or more press releases
- a backgrounder and/or fact sheet on the subject
- photograph(s)
- brochure(s)
- copies of any available article reprints
- transcript of any interviews or speeches
- repro(s) of any relevant ads
- CD-ROM, if appropriate
- other – anything that helps explain or promote the subject

Basically the content of the kit should be assembled or created to convey the best impression, providing media with whatever information is needed.

A press kit containing less than three pieces is probably too light to make much of an impression on an editor, writer or producer, or to provide enough Information to generate an interesting, colorful, or detailed story. More than seven pieces is probably overkill. So a totally arbitrary, but good number of elements to include in a press kit is probably five: two press releases, a fact sheet, backgrounder, and a speech transcript or an annual report or a reprint of an article from a non-competing publication to the one being approached.

Remember the objective. The press kit's purpose is to provide a summary of information that will serve as a briefing for someone about to conduct an interview or create a piece on a particular subject. It should be user-friendly, easy to read, and include detailed information. For the writer, it is, yet again, a form of storytelling.

What has a writer to be bombastic about?
Whatever good a man may write is the consequence of accident,
luck, or surprise, and nobody is more surprised than an honest
writer when he makes a good phrase or says something truthful.
— **Edward Dahlberg**

A writer never has a vacation.
For a writer life consists of either writing or thinking about writing.
— **Eugene Ionesco**

Rewriting ripens what you've written.
— **Duane Alan Hahn**

Topic 10: Research, Fact-checking, Plagiarism, Citations, Ethics

If some subjects or topics in this book justify having entire books about them, this chapter might warrant five individual books. In fact, separate volumes have been written about each subject area, but for purposes of providing an overview of their implications for writers, they have been brought together in one chapter because each has an integral connection to the others. Hopefully the connection will be obvious.

Research is a broad term and is often used very loosely. Companies such as the Gallup Organization; ACNielsen Corporation; Opinion Research Corp.; the Pew Research Center, and a number of other firms are real research organizations that conduct polling, surveys, studies and analyses that are recognized as authoritative and credible. Colleges, universities, and many media organizations conduct research using similarly recognized methodology to produce worthwhile factual reports that are also accepted for their accuracy and integrity. Unfortunately, many organizations exist to create research that will provide its sponsors with whatever conclusions they desire and, particularly in the Internet age, such misinformation is circulated and cited with alarming repetition.

Trend-shops observe students in a mall for a period of time and generate reports on their interests or buying habits, as well as what their future purchases will be. They are usually wrong. Many focus groups, test groups, and screenings are intentionally designed and include participants predisposed to a particular conclusion. Some individuals will ask a group for a show of hands or a round of applause regarding an opinion and attempt to pass it off as research. It isn't.

Most people have heard someone use the phrase, "I've conducted my own research in this area," which essentially means asking opinions over a period of time in various locations and concluding the majority of responses is representative of a much larger group. It almost certainly is not. The same is also true of the countless instances when opinions are offered as facts, typically preceded by phrases such as "everyone knows" or "it is widely accepted that..." or "reasonable people agree on this," when in truth these rhetorical devices are being used to influence or persuade without any basis in fact for their positions.

Real research is science, whether it is in chemical experimentation or eliciting information from carefully selected numbers of people having specific demographic or psychographic characteristics.

For writers, research means studying authoritative, credible material from which facts can be drawn and careful differentiation can be made from opinions.

Writers are called upon to write on a variety of subjects about which they cannot possibly know enough to produce good work without the benefit of research. Make certain that facts cited or information serving as the basis for written work is reliable, not simply drawn from Internet sources that trade in opinions or data unverified by a credible authority.

Opinions are worth citing as long as they are identified as such. But until proven to be correct, they are still opinions. Such small matters as the origin of the universe can be said to come under this heading.

While an encyclopedia would be held up as a reliable and authoritative source, technology and the culture of the times have changed that. Web sites and books offered as the "people's encyclopedia" – of which Wikipedia is perhaps the largest and best known – is a great source of information, but not all of it has been substantiated to be correct. Publications and Web sites that invite people to submit or post what they know on virtually any topic can be useful in collecting data, but until it is validated by some authoritative or scientific source or reference, it remains only "raw data" and should be referenced with care and qualification, if at all. To do otherwise is rather like looking at someone else's paper for a test answer and using that answer without knowing if it is incorrect. Just because information was drawn from an outside source does not mean it is accurate. Mistakes happen, but when they are copied by others, the results can be costly. A problem with modern Internet technology is that errors are repeated, archived, and cited by some people years after an original error has been removed or corrected.

Fact-checking is a self-explanatory term that might be considered research after-the-fact. It involves verification of comments, quotations, and references within a body of writing. While some media organizations employ fact-checkers, most rely on the writer to perform this function, which can require considerable resources and diligence.

Apart from the obvious, fact-checking is important in that writers who are not, or were not, trained reporters are more likely to make ethical or factual mistakes and checked copy is more likely to avert serious, sometimes costly, problems, such as lawsuits or severe damage to reputations when writers of media companies are discredited. In recent years, some of the largest and most prestigious media organizations, including CBS News, CNN, the *New York Times*, and the *New Republic*, suffered damage to their reputations for using material that could have been corrected by fact-checking.

Michael Kelly, who edited some of the erroneous *New Republic* stories, took responsibility himself, rather than blaming the magazine's fact-checkers, noting "Any fact-checking system is built on trust.... If a reporter is willing to fake notes, it defeats the system. Anyway, the real vetting system is not fact-checking but the editor."

235

Nonetheless, a writer who pays careful attention to such details can build a reputation for professionalism, rather than take a hit.

Plagiarism is something pretty much everyone involved with writing is warned about from middle school days. So why then, despite what must be a basic understanding by virtually all who have ever written – a simple matter of what's right or wrong – is it still an issue?

The answers run from innocent mistakes to misunderstandings to simple attempts to cut corners and save time by lifting other people's work, from small passages to larger excerpts to entire columns, concepts, ideas, or treatments. No one seems to challenge that plagiarism is theft and that it's wrong. Recent high profile cases involving one writer using another writer's work have been resolved based on questions of intent – relatively innocent errors involving inadvertently uncredited research. As a justification, that explanation might sell and get a writer a pass, but damage is always done as some people will continue to wonder if it was truly an innocent error or something more. Better to err on the side of caution and check research methods and material to avoid event the hint of unethical or unprofessional conduct. To credit someone for the use of his or her work is the professional thing to do and does not diminish the efforts of those who use the material of others.

Citations of course refer to the actual process of crediting the work of others that is used in creating a new work. Citations are references to books, articles, letters, Web pages, interviews, or other published or unpublished work with sufficient detail to identify the item, giving due credit or acknowledging the influence of other works. Media companies, publishers, and learning institutions have differing requirements as to citation formats. Writers are advised to investigate which format is preferred or required before submitting work.

Citations of a book generally include at least the author, book title, publisher, and date of publication. Citations of a journal or magazine article typically include at least the author, article title, publication title, volume, page number, and date of publication.

Citations of a work on the Internet, understandably the fastest-growing and most complex area for referencing, usually include at least the URL and a date when the work was accessed with, ideally, the date the material was originally posted.

Ethics is defined in most dictionaries simply as moral principles, or as rules of conduct recognized in respect to a class of human actions of a particular group or culture.

Ethics also used to be a much simpler issue in simpler times. It meant knowing the difference between right and wrong, appropriate and inappropriate conduct. It's the difference between professionalism and a lack of professionalism. What is that difference? We know it when we see it and we really know it when we experience it. Today the term "situational ethics" is used quite liberally and applied to suggest that, under certain circumstances, actions deemed unethical would be acceptable. It is at such times that it seems appropriate to invoke the expression "a slippery slope."

Different professions interpret the concept as "applied ethics" or an area in which interpretation might allow some wiggle room.

Reality should hold that if writers understand plagiarism, the Golden Rule, the Ten Commandments, and what acts or types of acts are illegal, what constitutes unethical behavior is something of a no-brainer. If, on the other hand, the writer tends to be inclined toward finding exemptions, loopholes, or other areas where rules concerning the differences between right and wrong don't apply, devoting more space to the subject here won't matter.

In any moment of decision, the best thing you can do is the right thing. The worst thing you can do is nothing.
— **Theodore Roosevelt**

Topic 11: The Creative Brief

Some writers consider the creative brief a road map. A marketing plan is also a road map, as is a PR plan. Soon, in this language of metaphors, only road maps will not be compared to road maps. A creative brief is, in fact, the core document for a project, defining the project, enabling the project plan to be developed, and remaining as the main point of reference during the development process to keep the project on track.

Creative Briefs are the best way to make certain that the outcome of a project is as it was intended to be. It gives the team a clear picture of what to build, who they are talking to, and what they need to accomplish. A good brief also leads to more effective ads.

It was noted earlier that it's difficult to meet expectations if one doesn't know what the expectations are. Many creative projects begin without a clear sense of what is expected between those requesting the project and the creative team charged with developing and delivering it. This can result in time lost and costly – as well as needless – reworking of material. A creative brief solves that problem by establishing an outline and a working plan for the creative team.

Note how much a creative brief resembles a marketing plan or PR plan.

1. Identify the target audience for the brief.
2. Prepare a situation analysis on issues or challenges to be addressed.
3. Identify the objective of the brief or plan.
4. Note the project's unique selling proposition (USP) that makes it different.

5. Determine the strategy to meet the objective.

6. Determine how much the audience already knows about the subject.

7. Note what subjects, if any, should be avoided.

8. Write a single sentence through all the clutter that addresses the subject.

9. Establish other major points to be communicated.

10. Determine the best media to reach the target audience.

11. Evaluate secondary audiences, as well as secondary media.

12. Note what products, projects, or collateral are to be part of the effort.

13. Consider if any modifications are necessary to make them compatible.

14. Note design objectives, any special circumstances, or mandatory elements.

15. Create a deadline for completion of the project.

16. Confirm the budget approved for the project.

17. Note who will be responsible for various phases of the project.

18. Establish who has final approval authority.

Most programs or projects need a plan – some type of document that describes what will be done, for whom, in what time frame, at what cost, and what special problems or considerations need to be addressed. Whether the document is ultimately called an outline, a plan, a road map, or a creative brief, it will help keep the project focused, moving ahead, and hopefully, free of any jams or unforeseen obstacles. Please drive carefully.

Being a writer means having homework for the rest of your life.
— **Lawrence Kasdan**

Topic 12: Writing Proposals, Résumés, and Cover Letters

Proposals are written presentations used to win approval and secure funding for projects, to receive grants and to land new accounts. Résumés are written statements of one's credentials prepared for the purpose of presenting them as reasons to be considered for sought-after jobs. Both require cover letters that must not repeat the contents of their accompanying documents, yet must make persuasive arguments as to why the writer should get what he or she is requesting. Each are very different pieces, yet the link is clear.

Because a proposal can be for so many different things, let's keep this outline fairly generic, yet specific in form.

It should be assumed that the reader of the proposal is busy, impatient, skeptical, and has no reason to want to give the proposal consideration. This crabby person is faced with more requests than Don Corleone on his daughter's wedding day. Even reading through the proposals is a chore. So get to the point. To start, the proposal should have:

- a title
- a date
- its author's name
- a brief introduction
- a summary paragraph that asks for approval

In between the introduction and the summary, it should answer ten questions:

1. What is the objective of the proposal (What do you want to do)?
2. Why is it a good idea (How do you justify the idea presented)?
3. How much will it cost?
4. How long will it take to complete what's being proposed?
5. How does the proposed offer relate to the interests of the parties involved?
6. What benefit will result from approval of the proposal?
7. What has already been done in this area to date?
8. How do you plan to do it?
9. How will the results be tracked and evaluated?
10. Why should you, rather than someone else, be chosen for this?

How long should the proposal be? An excellent question. The answer is: only as long as it needs to be. What some people can never seem to understand is that people can immediately recognize if a proposal or a résumé is padded – that is, loaded with extraneous information that the writer thinks will be more impressive if it comes in bulk. It won't. Proposals and résumés are two documents where quality beats quantity every time.

Here are guidelines:

- A one-page document looks as if not much thought went into it.

- A document of more than 10 pages, unless it is packed with solid, interesting and useful information, will probably turn off the reader with its excessive length.

- Something between two and eleven pages is probably the right length.

Next comes the most important point: why you? Other people want the account, the grant, the funding, the project, the job… so, why you? Remember when writing proposals or résumés or letters or ad copy or press releases that the reader has one overriding question: *What's in it for me?*

For the writer to get the business, the funding, or the job it must be noted clearly and concisely how the reader of the document will be better off by selecting the person or group presenting the document.

A popular college entrance interview question is: *how will this school community benefit from having you here?* That's a great question and it is the one grantors, funders, employers, and decision makers want answered, even when they aren't sure how to ask it.

Experience and creative thinking help, but the proposal or résumé that avoids focusing on how really swell the writer is, and instead emphasizes how the reader and his or her organization will be better for having the writer on board, is the proposal or résumé that gets the nod.

A résumé is a proposal – a pitch to win an interview. A résumé is also an ad.

Don't simply write what you have done. Make the same assertion a good ads makes: a claim that the person who buys this product will get specific, direct benefits. Let the prospective employer know the writer has what it takes to be successful and, in so doing, the organization he or she joins will reap the rewards.

The résumé is a relatively generic necessary job history, but it is also an ad for the writer.

The cover letter is an opportunity for directness, informality, creativity, even a chance to show a sense of humor or a particular bit of knowledge unique to the writer. Every proposal and every résumé is about showing that its writer is different. To that end, the cover letter should complement, not duplicate the accompanying résumé. Its purpose is to interpret the data-oriented, factual job history with a personal touch. A cover letter is often the earliest written contact with a potential employer, creating a critical first impression. It is the cover letter that can determine whether or not a proposal or a résumé gets read. Let it reflect a person with a purpose.

The writer must believe that what he is doing
is the most important thing in the world.
And he must hold to this illusion even when he knows it is not true.
— **John Steinbeck**

First, I do not sit down at my desk to put into verse something
that is already clear in my mind. If it were clear in my mind,
I should have no incentive or need to write about it.
We do not write in order to be understood,
we write in order to understand.
— **Robert Cecil Day-Lewis**

Endless conflicts. Endless misunderstanding. All life is that.
Great and little cannot understand one another.
— **H.G. Wells**

Topic 13: Newsletters

Walt Disney was famous for creating Mickey Mouse and Donald Duck, Pluto, Goofy, and an entire library of cartoons, then feature-length films, then a long-running TV series, then a theme park, and another theme park, and another, and a record company, a book publishing company, a couple of magazines, lines of clothing and hundreds of toys – all tied to his other enterprises – plus a few hotels and a cruise line. He also dabbled in real estate.

What does this have to do with newsletters?

This: Walt Disney directed the thousands of people in his employ that everything the company produced had to do two things: educate and entertain. Whether it was the Mickey Mouse Club, The Little Mermaid or Space Mountain, it had to educate and entertain.

So in the Internet age, when everyone seems to be on information overload, how does one write for or publish a newsletter that anyone will want to read? First, take a tip from the late genius Mr. Disney and demand that the newsletter, whether offered online or in a traditional, soon-to-be-antiquated printed paper format, not only educate and entertain, but inform, and persuade readers to participate in something that engages them with the subject, company, or product.

That last point is because most, if not all, newsletters produced are either consciously or unconsciously public relations vehicles and, besides awareness, the point of a public relations effort is to persuade people to buy, support, subscribe, contribute, or otherwise identify with a subject.

Consider in the first decade of the 21st century what people are concerned about, talking about, and reading about:

- Global warming
- War
- Election politics
- The economy (as related to personal needs, such as income and the prices of gas, food, college…)
- Health care
- Faith
- Humanity, as in kindness, understanding, helping people
- YouTube, MySpace, Facebook
- Paris Hilton, Lindsay Lohan, Britney Spears, the Apple iPhone, personal computers

With newspapers, magazines, television, radio, direct mail, and the Internet, getting people to read newsletters – much less getting good people to write for them – is a challenge.

Traditional subscribers must be offered information that is perceived as important to them.

Yet, if Harry Potter could prove books can still not only sell, but actually be read to the tune of more than 350 million copies(!), and if the same Harry Potter's fifth-in-a-series movie could post box office grosses of some $190 million in its first five days of release, and if *Dancing with the Stars* and *American Idol* can bring tens of millions of people back to their TV screens… newsletters are far from over.

Writers must write newsletters to educate and entertain, encourage debate and controversy, take tough stands, recognize talent. Newsletters today are competing for readership and interest with everything else printed. Newsletters must:

- know the audience – who's reading, who cares…
- give the audience what it wants and enjoys reading
- stay fresh with bright features, photos, and color

- keep it personal – it's not the *New York Times*; loosen up
- be bright and bold (as with newspapers, headlines set the tone)
- be reader friendly – if it's online, make it easy to scan
- include lively information worth sharing
- show and tell – include "conversation starters" and print feedback comments.

Newsletters are typically associated with someone's company, school, industry, a cause, or a particular group. Skip the "inside baseball" stuff most people don't read and give it a warm, friendly, personal feeling like a conversation with a friend.

As with any other communication medium, content rules. If a newsletter is interesting and entertaining, people will read it. Sometimes it's all in the packaging. Instead of a "newsletter" try issuing a "special report" or "an executive summary" or an "organization alert." In other words… a newsletter, but call it something else.

A professional writer is an amateur who didn't quit.
— **Richard Bach**

I write when I'm inspired,
and see to it that I'm inspired at nine o'clock every morning.
— **Peter De Vries**

Topic 14: Writing for Radio and TV

Mention writing for radio and people think the discussion is about writing ad copy for a carpet company. Before TV, radio was comedy, drama, music, and much more. Radio made famous *Little Orphan Annie*, *Sky King*, and the Golden Age of Comedy that included comedy legends Bob Hope, Jack Benny, and Burns & Allen. Drama was *Dragnet* and Orson Wells' classic *War of the Worlds*.

In the 21st century radio has reinvented itself: talk radio is powerful and satellite radio, still in its infancy, has people paying for what is available up and down the listening band without charge. *A Prairie Home Companion* and *Grand Ol' Opry* still attract loyal audiences and NPR collects millions of dollars annually from listeners who choose to pay for it even though they don't really need to.

Writing for radio still affords opportunities, particularly in news, talk, comedy, and sports. Free Speech Radio offers writers this advice:

- Keep it short and fast!

- Every second counts. Write short sentences, one basic idea in each sentence.

- Try to cram information into peoples' ears, one short line at a time.

- Long, complicated sentences full of big words don't make people sound smart.

- Say what you mean, throw away all unnecessary words, and try to maintain a conversational style.

- Put the subject at the front of each sentence, using the formula: (subject) + (verb) + (object) + (...all other stuff).

247

- Long, newspaper-style sentences should be broken up into smaller sentences.

- Sentences should be written in the positive, as opposed to the negative sense, as often as possible.

- Avoid using "not", "no", "don't", "doesn't", "won't", etc.

- Write in the present tense, whenever possible.

- Start and end stories with a person, a personal story, an illustrative anecdote... something that the listener can understand and relate to immediately.

- Remind listeners of the subject of a story as it goes along and near the end.

Moving from radio to TV writing is intimidating to some writers because of the real and perceived power associated with the medium. Television Newswriting Workshop's Mervin Block offers this advice to TV writers:

1. Start strong. Well begun is half done.
2. Read – and understand – your source copy.
3. Underline or circle key facts.
4. Think. Don't write yet. Think.
5. Write the way you talk.
6. Apply the rules for broadcast news writing.
7. Have the courage to write simply.
8. Refrain from wordy warm-ups.
9. Put attribution before assertion.
10. Go with S-V-O: subject – verb - object.
11. Limit a sentence to one idea.
12. Use short words and short sentences.
13. Use familiar words in familiar combinations.
14. Humanize your copy. And localize it.

15. Activate your copy: use active voice – and action verbs.

16. Avoid a first sentence whose main verb is any form of to be.

17. Avoid a first sentence whose main verb is may, could, seems.

18. Use present tense verbs where appropriate.

19. Put your sentences in a positive form.

20. Don't start with a quotation or a question.

21. Use connectives (and, also, but, so, because) to link sentences.

22. Put the word or words you wish to stress at the end of your sentence.

23. Use contractions – with caution.

24. Pep up your copy with words like new, now, but, says.

25. Watch out for I, we, our, here, up, down.

26. Omit needless words. (Is every word necessary? If it's not necessary to leave it in, it is necessary to leave it out.)

27. Hit only the highlights.

28. Don't parrot source copy.

29. Place the time element, if you need one, after the verb.

30. When in doubt, leave it out.

31. Don't raise questions you don't answer.

32. Read your copy aloud. If it sounds like writing, rewrite it.

33. The art of writing lies in rewriting what you've already rewritten.

34. Pray. And polish your résumé.

With the expansion of the number of television stations made available through cable and satellite TV systems, reruns of *Gunsmoke* and *I Love Lucy* will only go so far. From news programming to talk shows, documentaries, sports, and programs on cooking, travel, and hobbies, opportunities for writers are more, not less, despite the universe reportedly shifting its interest to streaming video and the Internet.

If you want to see television stations panic,
go to a town where the newspapers are on strike.
— **Unattributed quote**

Topic 15: Internet Writing: Web Sites and Blogs

By now it's not a very original observation that the Internet and the World Wide Web have changed most things in American life, such as how people buy, sell, shop, teach, learn, and communicate. In many respects the changes took hold so rapidly that there was barely time to call it a phenomenon.

Computers have been around for generations, not only automating, but being cited for millions of errors humans couldn't blame on their dogs, but the "personal computer" truly came into its own in the early 1990s. Today no business and relatively few families don't own, have access to, or make use of technology in some form. Modern life seems as much about uploads, downloads, podcasts, Facebook, My Space, and YouTube as it is about anything else.

Commercially, the term "revolution" seems an understatement. And for a writer, the change has not been slight. Despite e-books being a highly touted non-event, books and magazines maintain their places (for the time being) and newspapers hang on, circulation dropping in no small part because new technology has both changed the economics of the industry and made possible alternatives and content choices not available in even the recent past. It is against such a backdrop that writers find new options and outlets online and elsewhere. But with the change comes education, reeducation or, at a minimum, a shifting of the literary gears.

We read differently from screens so we must write differently for them.

As more eyes turn to personal computer screens and handheld devices, writers must adjust. If writing for a Web site or a blog:

- Present your most salient points at the top of the Web page.
- Write short paragraphs.
- White space helps display your words; write in 'copy blocks' of no more than 30-word paragraphs.
- Write simple sentences.
- Use one idea per sentence.
- Keep sentences to less than 17 words.
- Use the present or present perfect tense.
- Be direct. The informality of the Web suggests a friendly, more personal tone (such as using we and you instead of the student, the doctor, etc.)
- Use positive terminology, as in "I'm well" instead of "not bad."
- Know your audience. Present material in a format readers expect.
  1) Know the Web site or blog's purpose.
  2) Know who makes up the audience and what type of person is attracted to the site.
  3) Be clear about where and how what's written for the Web will be used, as comments and excerpts can be modified or taken without permission or knowledge. Debates over intellectual property are likely to go on for decades.
- Reread what you have written before sending it to your reader. Changes can sometimes be a hassle and once the words are "out there" they are out there forever.

The Internet has clearly matured during the first decade of the 21st century, though it is equally clear that, in many respects, it is still in its infancy. Is it possible to experience a mature infancy? If it is, the Internet is the place it will happen.

The "big shakeout" has yet to occur and the 'net is working through some growing pains with tens of millions of Web sites and blogs no one sees. Knowledgeable people still insist "content is king" and good ideas and good work will always find a place, if not dominate the Internet.

The comedian Mort Sahl many years ago titled a comedy album *The Future Lies Ahead*. It's one of those titles that can initially slide by before people express their delayed reaction (usually, "Duh" or "ya' think?"). But when it comes to Internet communication and opportunities for writers of all genres, the future is here... and ahead, again... more than ever.

A Writer's Lexicon

A Writer's Lexicon of
Words & Terms

There is so much to know. Some people devote their lives to the pursuit of knowledge and never stop learning. Certainly some people feel it's enough to acquire a mass of knowledge in a particular subject area and position themselves as experts, believing they know – if not all there is to know – all they need to know.

Many of the best writers rely on inspiration and talent to write; others need a plan. Serious writers understand the importance of research, as well as imagination, and creativity (not the same thing) in various combinations in exploring different aspects of many subjects.

Many writers are driven by a love of learning. The joy in writing is, in part, the exploration and discovery of new places and things and new ways of looking at what they thought they already knew well. It's not unusual to find writers' homes filled with books – wall to wall, floor to ceiling, room to room. Visitors invariably ask, "Have you read all these?" A momentary pause follows before some writers answer simply, "Yes," while others reply, "No, but I hope to." It is the desire to know more that makes many writers want to read, as well as write, as writing is about sharing what is known.

This book cannot even approach exposing an aspiring or seasoned writer to a fraction of what is "out there." Courses in composition, deconstruction, and the myriad of other facets, disciplines, exercises, and aspects of good writing fill volumes. Writers are encouraged to keep learning, to revisit the rules of structure and language, and remember the advice of T.S. Eliot, "It's not wise to violate the rules until you know how to observe them."

Paradigms, Clichés, Tropes, Conversance, Convergence

You love to read. You thought of yourself as educated – or at least pretty smart. You are reading an interesting article in the Sunday newspaper or a delightful novel by Peter Mayle or the newest biography of Truman Capote when – Bam! Choke! Cough! – you are stopped by a word you don't know. Perhaps it's Latin. Or, maybe this time it's French. What the hell does sui generis mean? What is or was the Rosetta Stone?

Clearly the person writing this expects you to know. Does everyone else reading this know what those things are? You wonder if the words are truly integral to the piece or if the writer is showing off and you should just roll over them and keep reading. But it stays with you and makes you crazy until something happens to distract you. Then, later, between remembering there was a word that stopped you (though you can't now recall what it was) and being just a bit annoyed with yourself because, as a writer yourself, you think you are supposed to know this stuff… your brain starts to itch.

A good vocabulary is useful to a writer – some would argue it is essential. But if the objective of writing is to convey information, entertainment or emotion, it follows that the reader must also have a command of the language at least equal to that of the writer. Again we are drawn back to the point that a writer should know whom he or she is writing for and choose words that most effectively communicate in ways the reader will understand and appreciate.

Writers – at least some writers – are drawn to writing for a love a words and the knowledge that a grouping of words can come together to convey a thought, a message, a story, sometimes touching or powerful, and be informative, useful, and occasionally brilliant. These groupings of words change people's lives, whether they come from the pen (or typewriter or word processor) of William Shakespeare or Woody Allen – both of whom have inspired people with their special ways of putting together words.

Writers are readers. Research indicates that perhaps the one characteristic most people who write have in common is a love of reading. It is more than something to do in a waiting room. Reading, for all its joy, is serious business. The words the writer chooses and the reader reads must be more than random (which, incidentally, has broken out of the pack to be suddenly popular and somewhat overused as a word in the early years of the twenty-first century).

Here's the important thing about words and writing: the more words you know, the greater your vocabulary (duh). But to go a step beyond stating the obvious, the greater your vocabulary, the better for you to express yourself – what you have to say and what you mean. The better your ability to express yourself, the greater your skill is and will be as a writer.

What you do about observing rules of grammar and punctuation and whether or not you choose to leave your participles dangling is a separate matter. Know the words and what they mean in order to better tell the story.

One book review alone in the *New York Times* included the words bourgeois, demoiselle, supercilious, vertiginous, epicurean, and gustatory. It's a safe bet that most readers of those six words were unfamiliar with at least half of them. So why were they bundled into, not an intellectual's professional journal, but one of the most widely read English-language daily newspaper around the world? Only the writer and editor might know for certain. But what about the reader?

When S.I. Hayakawa wrote *Use the Right Word: A Modern Guide to Synonyms*, he wasn't just trying to go *Roget's Thesaurus* one better. He meant what he wrote. Using the "right" word makes for better reading than choosing a word to impress the reader (or yourself) or to appear more stylish. "Use the right word," Hayakawa said. It wasn't just a book title. It was simple, yet great advice.

So what's the deal then with Abraxas? Is it a word? A person? A place? Or just the curious title of an early popular album by Santana – an album that a million people bought and listened to without knowing what its title meant, if indeed, it meant anything at all?

And now that you've sung Auld Lang Syne once a year for a few decades, shouldn't you learn what you are singing?

What of "the perilous fight o'er the ramparts we watched…"? What's a rampart? These might not be the most important questions in the grand scheme of things, but a writer should know.

Often people have heard or read words they are familiar with, though they don't know quite what the words mean. Sometimes a word's meaning can be understood by making an assumption based on the sentence or the context in which it is used. And that assumption might be correct, but a writer – particularly a journalist – can't afford to guess what a word means; he or she must know it.

The Power of Words

Children have a rhyme that goes, "Sticks and stones may break my bones, but words will never hurt me." This small bit of wisdom was also the inspiration for a great Ray Charles song in the 1960s. But alas, as wisdom, it falls short. Words can hurt, as well as disappoint people and change lives in significant ways. The originator of the phrase no doubt was unfamiliar with the British novelist Edward George Bulwer Lytton's famous quote that, "the pen is mightier than the sword." Today, it could be said, that goes double for the word processor.

Consider the person hearing or reading the words, "You didn't get the job" or "We've decided to go with someone else" or "We're not giving you the loan" or "I love someone else" or "I'm leaving" or "I never loved you" or "You're a lousy lover."

Ouch! Some people would probably prefer being pelted with sticks and stones to hearing any of those short, simple, yet very hurtful words. Words can embarrass and humiliate. Rumors can destroy businesses and lives.

Conversely, words can change lives in very positive ways – "I love you" or "Marry me" or "You got the job" or "Your loan is approved" or "The operation was a complete success" – and bring varying degrees of joy or elation. Imagine getting a note from someone saying he or she can't live without you. Whether the note is from your true love or your boss, it carries quite a punch.

Stephen King writes about writing being a form of telepathy – where a writer can picture something, describe it in words on a page, and a reader, reading those words years later will get the same mental picture the writer had – a thought communicated through time and space.

Numbers, as well as letters, add power to pronouncements. By noting that there are "three primary reasons" or "a 10 best list" and numbering each point, their importance appears to be greater. The same is true for points listed singularly as point A; point B; point C; etc. Such devices as numbering and lettering points in a list direct a reader's focus with suggestions of their relative weight or value.

> *Handle them carefully,*
> *for words have more power than atom bombs.*
> — **Pearl Strachan**

> *Broadly speaking, the short words are the best,*
> *and the old words best of all.*
> — **Sir Winston Churchill**

> *Think like a wise man*
> *but communicate in the language of the people.*
> — **William Butler Yeats**

> *If you wouldn't write it and sign it, don't say it.*
> — **Earl Wilson**

The New Paradigm

Composer Peter Allen wrote what many people were finding to be true: "Everything old is new again." When writers look for a new way to describe the latest societal change, some create new words that are hybrids or acronyms for terms, while others sometimes find the dustiest parts of the library, with arcane and antiquated terms, is a good place to look for something "new." For example, the *American Heritage Dictionary* defines this word this way:

paradigm n. One that serves as a pattern or model.

1. A set or list of all the inflectional forms of a word or of one of its grammatical categories: the paradigm of an irregular verb.

2. A set of assumptions, concepts, values, and practices that constitutes a way of viewing reality for the community that shares them, especially in an intellectual discipline.

As best it can be determined, the word paradigm first appeared in the English language some time in the 15th century and was used to describe "an example or pattern." It was not however, introduced into everyday conversation and common usage in the United States until the late 1970s, when the revolution occurred in technology and describing a new program or practices or concepts or model or system or standard or prototype did not have a distinctive enough ring to emphasize the uniqueness of the form and the enormous implications it represented.

Technology did not just bring about something new and exciting, it had created a "new paradigm" that would alter the standard, model, concept, and pattern of how things would operate – of how life itself would change. And people who work with words must take note of the change, as it is reflective of the "new" – even if the word to describe it dates back six centuries.

An epidemic is an outbreak of a contagious disease that spreads rapidly and widely or a rapidly spread, growth, or development. A pandemic is an epidemic that spreads over a very wide area.

How are there two terms functionally distinct from one another? The answer is they are not; it is a matter of choice as to which word describes what the writer or speaker wants to describe with the proper inflection.

The point being that a thesaurus has its place and a writer must determine how best to describe a subject and whether or not the paradigm is new… or just the word used to describe it. Usually, it's about the words.

Don't use words too big for the subject.
Don't say "infinitely" when you mean "very";
otherwise you'll have no word left when you want to talk about
something really infinite.

— C.S. **Lewis**

Clichés, Catch Phrases, and Old Sayings

Linguistics is the scientific or humanistic study of language and literature.

The official version goes like this:

- a **cliché** is a trite, stereotyped expression;

- a **figure of speech** is language used in a figurative or non-literal sense;

- a **proverb** is a short pithy saying that expresses a basic truth;

- a **saying** is something that is said (such as a proverb);

- an **adage** is a traditional saying that reflects a common experience or observation; and

- an **expression** is a mode or means of expressing an idea, opinion, or thought.

So, what's the difference between an adage, a proverb, an expression, a cliché, a figure of speech, and a saying? The distinction today is blurred enough to be virtually irrelevant. The fact is that the terms are pretty much used interchangeably when describing what is basically a very familiar or overused statement, which may or may not carry an element of wisdom or truth. Sometimes expressions are only reflective of conversational patterns that suggest more the phrase of the month – influenced, for example, by popular culture – than something that will survive the seasons.

Since the earliest of classroom recollections, students have been warned not to use clichés when writing or speaking. Perhaps referring to the cliché as an adage would have been a way of skirting the admonition, but teacher was only trying to be helpful.

Consider the number of people who have actually had first-hand experiences that allow them to judge the level of fun that might be had in a barrel of moneys, or who shot fish in a barrel or felt a need to single out a large number of anything and shake a stick at it. Obsessive personalities can search out the origin of these phrases, but the point is that many years later and well removed from these origins, people still use the phrases without knowledge – or even a thought – of their meanings or relevancy to the subjects at hand.

There are thousands of clichés and expressions and most people would admit to having their own special favorites, as well as several that annoy them most. Writers should care.

When used as they are, to the extreme, many of these phrases are merely glib or tiresome, though some are invoked with a near-reverence, as if they are imbued with a unique or profound wisdom. The main reason, however, that writers should strive to avoid using such expressions is not only because they are overused, but because their familiarity could invite associations the audience might have with the words or phrases that diminishes the power or value a writer hopes the words will carry.

The bitterest tears shed over graves
are for words left unsaid and deeds left undone.
— **Harriet Beecher Stowe**

Knowing Tropes

A trope is a figure of speech using words in non-literal ways, such as a metaphor.

While the point of this book is not to review grammatical terms and their uses which should have been learned in elementary school, the fact is that many people did not learn, or have forgotten, information that might not be important in everyday life for everyone, but is important to the person who needs to write or chooses to write, in order to communicate more effectively.

The familiar word "literally" emphasizes that what follows it is being referred to or discussed in very exacting and true terms, as opposed to "figuratively," which is not actual, but a comparative, exaggerated, or flippant reference. Non-literal is another term for figurative, the opposite of literal and, in linguistics, it is called a trope, which can take several forms:

- Metonymy is a trope through proximity or correspondence, such as referring to something the U.S. President did as "the actions of the White House";

- Irony, which would use a trope to imply the opposite of the usual meaning, such as describing a disaster as "good news";

- Metaphor, which compares something for the sake of example, without using the words "like" or "as" to explain it;

- Synecdoche, relating to metonymy and metaphor by creating a play on words, such as calling workers hired hands; and

- Antanaclasis, a stylistic trope that repeats a single word.

So in linguistics, a trope is a rhetorical figure of speech that consists of an example or a play on words, using a word in a way other than what is considered its literal or normal form. A more complete and in-depth study of tropes would include the allegory, anacoenosis, anthemia, antiphrasis, antonomasia, aphorisms, aporia, apostrophe, archaism, auxesis, catachresis, circumlocution, erotema, euphemism, hysteron proteron, hyperbole, and innuendo.

The word trope itself is not as familiar as the term metaphor, but it can be useful for writers to know the words, terms, and how they apply, whether or not the words pop up often in everyday conversation. The writer should care.

As noted, linguistics is the scientific or humanistic study of language and literature.

English is a wonderful language. Despite its being derived from so many other languages (Latin, Greek, French, Italian, German, etc.), English draws upon the best of them for a language that is, at once, powerful, romantic, musical, and as specific as it needs to be – often perhaps too specific in the opinion of many who study English as a second or third language. In addition to the nouns, pronouns, verbs, adverbs, adjectives, and articles, consider the gerunds, participles, and the above noted cliché, figure of speech, proverb, saying, adage and expression, and add the…

- simile, a common figure of speech comparing two different things, and the
- euphemism, a softer expression substituted for one that is offensive or harsh.

Euphemisms and Oxymorons

Many writers find euphemisms – also referred to by the disparaging term "doublespeak" – to be one of the more interesting developments in the English language. *Webster's Dictionary* defines a euphemism as: the substitution of an agreeable or inoffensive expression for one that may offend or suggest something unpleasant. Some of the more common euphemisms are:

sanitary landfill	=	garbage dump
sanitation worker	=	garbage collector
pre-owned vehicles	=	used cars
powder room	=	toilet
visually impaired	=	blind
custodian	=	janitor
bathroom tissue	=	toilet paper

There are distinctions as to when euphemisms are employed to flatter someone or to be "politically correct". The type of euphemism described as doublespeak is language deliberately constructed to disguise or distort the actual meaning of terms. Such language is usually associated with government, military, or corporate institutions and is used by these entities to soften the negative public relations impact that would likely result from calling situations or occurrences what they are.

An example is a corporation using the term "downsizing" instead of announcing the firing of a significant number of employees; or the military describing torture as the use of "enhanced interrogation techniques;" or terms such as "wet work" to describe the act of assassinating someone.

And if coming up with euphemisms can be a stimulating challenge for a writer, that task is no less daunting for the oxymoron – the pairing of contradictory words (think "constant change" or "educated guess"). A popular Web site lists these among the most consistently popular oxymorons:

alone together

silent scream

living dead

same difference

taped live

plastic glasses

peace force

pretty ugly

head butt

working vacation

virtual reality

dodge ram

work party

jumbo shrimp

Whether trying to be irreverent, funny, satiric, or bluntly critical, the oxymoron is a device open to writers, to be used judiciously in order to make a point. Overindulgence in the use of this device becomes tiresome quickly.

Don't, Sir, accustom yourself to use big words for little matters.
— **Dr. Samuel Johnson**

Whatever words we utter should be chosen with care
for people will hear them and be influenced by them for good or ill.
— **Buddha**

Words Writers Should Know...

Writing is, as has been noted here several times in several places, about the words. This book includes a lexicon, though it is not a dictionary. Writers need a dictionary. This is also not a vocabulary-builder, though, to communicate effectively, writers need a good vocabulary.

Can simple people with limited language skills communicate and even write well? Yes. It's not necessary to be an intellectual or have the expansive vocabulary of the late erudite author and intellectual William F. Buckley, Jr. to be a good communicator or writer. But, as the saying goes, knowledge is power, so to communicate more effectively and write better, we must accept that knowledge is found in words – in reading, listening, thinking, speaking, writing, editing, and rewriting. These are all skills that will help anyone do well, and they are all skills within reach of everyone.

I am very proud that I am smart enough to get to the point.
— **Harry Truman**

The poet cannot invent new words every time, of course.
He uses the words of the tribe. But the handling of the word,
the accent, a new articulation, renew them.
— **Eugene Ionesco**

Here Are 208 Words Writers Should Know:

Everyone does not need to know every word in a language to be intelligent. A problem all too common, however, is when someone does not know a particular word or term and either skips over it or guesses at its meaning. Big mistake. Duplicity, for example, means lying, not duplicating; penultimate is not the same as ultimate, it means next to last. Misassumptions of the meaning of words happens everyday. This may not be an issue to many or even to most people, but writers should have a better command of words and their meanings than most people if their written work is to be effective and truly reflective of what they mean to communicate.

Most of these words can be found in a good dictionary, but many cannot. The problem with their being unlisted is that, despite being ignored by the likes of Webster or Funk & Wagnall, or American Heritage, they are words and terms likely to be found in today's newspaper or a general interest magazine or contemporary book. In fact, the author noted virtually all of these words appearing in mainstream media within a year prior to publication of this book. Readers are simply expected to know what these words mean, even when they are in French, German, Italian, Latin, or are only being dropped into the writing because a writer is showing-off.

If readers are reading these words, writers should know them as well and make his or her own judgment as to whether or not they belong in a story or an article (or even in the language) in order to effectively communicate what a writer wants to convey. Some of the words and terms (but not many) are the language of the business – the writer's business –words such as lead-time and lede, magalog, and kicker.

The most recent edition of the *Oxford English Dictionary* is 20 volumes and claims to have approximately 60 million words, including some 5,000 "new words" and nearly 2.5 million quotations. Most writers today can get by knowing somewhat fewer words than that. This is a start.

Abraxas – a name containing the Greek letters alpha, beta, rho, alpha, xi, alpha, sigma, which, as numerals, amounted to 365, and used to signify the supreme deity as ruler of the 365 heavens of the system; also a mystical word used as a charm.

abstemious – moderate or temperate

abstract – a synopsis of a piece of nonfiction writing

abstruse – difficult to understand

acrimony – bitterness; acerbity

ad hominem – appealing to prejudices; attacking an opponent's character rather than his or her argument

adulterate – falsify

adumbrate – symbolize or outline broadly

adverse – to oppose

advertorial – article or text created to resemble a newspaper editorial, though it is in fact a paid ad

affect – to influence or effect a change; to simulate

agonists – when used after a person's name (usually in a title) indicates the person is a combatant or one facing a struggle

AIDA – in writing, it refers to the motivating sequence, which holds that good writing (particularly in advertising and public relations) must motivate readers by generating attention, interest, desire and action regarding a subject

alfresco – outside in the open air

allegory – representation of abstract ideas or principles by characters, figures, or events; short moral story

alliteration - using the same consonant at the beginning of each stressed syllable in verse

273

alter ego – another side of oneself; a second self

altruism – selflessness

amanuensis – someone employed to take dictation or to copy a manuscript

ambiguous – open to having several possible meanings or interpretations; equivocal

ambient – surrounding

ambivalent – mixture of opposite feelings or attitudes

ameliorate – improve

anachronism – displaced in time

Augean stable – accumulation of corruption, filth almost beyond the man's power to remedy.

angst – anxiety or apprehension, often accompanied by depression

antediluvian – old-fashioned, obsolete

antithesis – against; direct contrast or exact opposition to something

apathy – a lack of feeling or concern

aphorism – short statement of principle

apocryphal – questionable authenticity

apocalypse – a revelation or prophecy; a universal or widespread disaster; destruction

apogee – the highest or most distant point; climax

apothegm – short pithy instructive saying

apotheosis – glorification

arcane – understood by very few

archetype – a model or first form; a prototype

arrant – obvious

assiduous – unceasing, persistent

assimilate – absorb

athenaeum – a library or other place for study and learning

augur – predict

auld lang syne – the times gone past; the good old days

axiom – an obvious truth; principle

bagatelle – plaything or trinket

bellicose – hostile

bifurcate – separate into two parts

bildungsroman – novel whose principal subject is the moral, psychological, and intellectual development of a usually youthful main character

blog – short for "Web log" a personal column or posting on the World Wide Web

Boswell – devoted admirer, student, and recorder of another's words and deeds

bourgeois – person belonging to the middle class or with attitudes marked by conformity

Byzantine – of or pertaining to the Byzantine Empire; (sometimes lowercase) elaborate scheming and intrigue, especially for gaining political power or favor

callow – immature; childish

canticle – song, chant, or hymn with words from Biblical text

caprice – impulsive change of mind (capricious – impulsive and unpredictable)

chapbook – small book or pamphlet containing poems, ballads, or stories

closing – in newspapers and magazines, the time at which the paper accepts no further material for publication

Columbia – the United States [in reference to Christopher Columbus]

conflate – to merge or fuse into one entity

conundrum – a paradoxical, insoluble, or difficult problem; a dilemma

cri de coeur – impassioned outcry, as in a protest

dateline – identifier at the beginning of a newspaper or magazine article or a press release that notes the date and the story's point of origin

deadline – set time for completion of an assignment

denouement – result

Diaspora – dispersion of a people from their original homeland

didactic – instructive

dialectic controversy – the exchange of arguments and counter-arguments respectively advocating propositions and counter-propositions

disambiguate – to establish a single grammatical or semantic interpretation

disingenuous – not straightforward or candid, giving a false impression of being honest

doppelgänger – ghostly double of a living person

dystopia – fictional oppressive authoritarian-ruled society; the opposite of utopia

egregious – obviously or noticeably bad

elegiac – expressing sorrow often for something past

enervate – weaken

ennui – boredom

epicene – effeminate

eponymous – to have the name of a person (e.g. Hilton Hotel)

erudite – knowledgeable or scholarly

eschatology – branch of theology concerned with the end of the world or of mankind

ethos – individuality

euphony – agreeable, pleasing and harmonious sounds

exegesis – an explanation or critical interpretation

existential – dealing with existence derived from experience; the experience of existence

exposition – technique of communicating information by explaining details or skillfully relating details at the beginning of an article or story

expurgate – remove objective portions

fact sheet – a basic, concise outline of the facts of a subject

fallacious – deceptive or misleading

fanzine – a fan magazine

faux pas – a mistake

flout – show contempt

folio – a sheet of paper folded to form four pages; an oversized book format; page numbers and/or a book's title, chapter title, and page numbers

Gnostic – pertaining to knowledge, especially esoteric knowledge of spiritual matters

gothic – in literature, style of fiction that emphasizes the grotesque, mysterious, desolate

haiku – a three line, seventeen syllable poem, usually about nature

hegemony – predominant influence of a single state, region, or group over others

ibid – Latin abbreviation for ibidem, meaning "in the same place"

iconoclast – one who attacks or destroys deeply held or cherished beliefs of traditions

idiom – language unique to a particular people or profession

image statement – at the close of press releases, a short identifying statement describing the person, company, or organization that is the author or subject of the document

imbue – permeate, saturate

inculcate – indoctrinate; teach through repetition

ineluctably – inevitable, unavoidable

inexorable – relentless

insouciant – indifferent; nonchalant

intrepid – fearless

itinerant – traveling from place to place, especially for work

inverted pyramid – a writing style in which the major points are presented in the first sentence or paragraph and details are elaborated in descending order of importance

irony – a figure of speech in which the intended meaning is the opposite of what's stated

jejune – immature; childish

jeremiad – a long and bitter complaint

junta – conspiracy

kicker – journalism term for a short, upbeat ending

kudos – praise

lacuna – blank space; a gap

lead (also written **lede**) – journalism term for the beginning of a story that "leads" readers into the main body

lead time – time between the media receiving content for publication and actually publishing it

lexicon – a type of dictionary or specialized vocabulary

libel – written or published defamation; injury to a person's name or reputation

licentious – lewd; disregarding accepted standards of morality

linguistics – the scientific or humanistic study of language and literature

logline – a one-sentence description of a TV script or screenplay

logos – spirit; animating force of the world

loquacious – wordy; talkative

magalog – a combination catalog and magazine

malaise – physical discomfort usually associated with depression

malevolent – evil

media – a plural term referring to communication disseminators, such as newspapers, magazines, radio, TV, and the Internet and persons who collectively comprise this group

median – halfway between two extremes

meta – beyond; self-referential, especially self-parody; reference that assumes it's understood

misanthrope – one who hates or mistrusts people in general

misogyny – hatred of women

motif – an idea or theme that recurs throughout a work

nascent – coming into existence

Nihilism – form of skepticism that denies all existence, believes all values are baseless and repudiates all theories of morality and religious belief; holds that life is meaningless

nonplussed – confused

non sequitur – statement that does not follow logically from what preceded it

obfuscate – confuse

obsequious – fawning

obtuse – lacking quickness of perception or intellect

Occam's Razor – the principle that the simplest of competing theories is likely the best

oeuvre – work or a collection of one's life's work

officious – intrusive or meddling

oligarchy – political system in which a few people control government

omnibus – numerous objects or items considered at once

onomatopoeia – a word whose sound represents a physical sound, such as sizzle or click

ostensibly – appearing to be so

outré – eccentric or bizarre

oxymoron – combined terms that contradict each other

pandemic – widespread or general

panglossian – naively optimistic

paradigm – a pattern or model; set of assumptions, concepts, values, or practices

paradox – statement or proposition that seems absurd or contradicts itself, but might be true

pathos – sadness; a quality that arouses emotions

pax – period of wide-ranging stability under a single dominant power

pedagogy – teaching; preparatory training or instruction

pejorative – having a disparaging, derogatory or belittling effect

penultimate – the next to last

pernicious – wicked or destructive

perspicacious – acutely insightful and wise

perverse – willfully determined to be or do the opposite of what is expected or desired

peruse – to study or read carefully

philippic – a bitter verbal attack

picaresque – term applied to stories related in satiric or humorous episodes

plagiarism – using the work of another without attribution, permission, or compensation and representing it as one's own

plebeian – member of the lower class; a coarse or vulgar person

plutocracy – a wealthy class controls a government

poetic license – privilege claimed by writers to deviate from established form to achieve a desired effect

polemic – an argument, especially refuting or attacking a specific opinion or doctrine

polyglot – speaking, writing, written in, or composed of several languages

polymorphous – having or assuming various forms

portmanteau – a word formed by joining two others and combining their meanings (smog is a blend of smoke and fog; motel combines motor and hotel; brunch is breakfast and lunch

postulate – to assume as a premise

precipice – brink of a disastrous situation; cliff with a vertical or overhanging face

propaganda – information disseminated by advocates or opponents of a particular issue, doctrine, or cause

proletarian – a worker

puerile – immature; childish

raison d'être – justification or reason for existing

rampart – barrier created to protect or defend; fortification

rectitude – integrity or righteousness

red herring – a diversion intended to distract attention from the main issue; also a reddish fish

reticent – restrained or reserved; reluctant; quiet

Rosetta Stone – found in Egypt, a stone with a trilingual inscription, a key to deciphering hieroglyphics of ancient Egypt

schadenfreude – pleasure derived from misfortunes of others

sanguine – cheerfully confident; optimistic

sectarian – narrow-minded; parochial; characteristic of a sect

secular – worldly rather than spiritual; not specifically aligned with a religion

semantics – scientific or philosophical study of words and their meanings

sentient – capable of feeling; conscious

sophistry – subtle, tricky, superficially plausible, but generally false method of reasoning

sub rosa – confidentially; privately

sui generis – one of a kind; unique

supercilious – arrogant

supernumerary – superfluous; extra

tactile – perceptible to touch; tangible

tendentious – holding a strong implicit point of view; partisan

terrestrial – a human being

torpor – mental or physical inactivity or insensibility; lethargy; apathy

troglodyte – reclusive, reactionary, out of date; brutish; curmudgeon

trope – a figure of speech using words in nonliteral ways, such as a metaphor

unctuous – affected, exaggerated, or insincere earnestness

ursprache (oorshprach) – a parent language (word that won the 2006 National Spelling Bee)

variorum – of different versions of a text, notes by various editors, scholars, and critics

veritas – truth

vernacular – standard native language of a country or region

vertiginous – revolving or whirling; dizzy; inclined to change quickly; unstable

verisimilitude – the quality of appearing to be true or real

xenophobia – a fear or hatred of foreigners

When you want to fool the world, tell the truth.
— **Otto von Bismarck**

Words, as is well known, are the great foes of reality.
— **Joseph Conrad**

The basic tool for the manipulation of reality is the manipulation of words. If you can control the meaning of words, you can control the people who must use the words.
— **Philip K. Dick**

Sources and Resources

Most of the material contained in this book is the author's own, though the quotes of many notable and celebrated persons were drawn from hundreds of books, articles, and references. Wikipedia was used on occasion to reference some things, but never without verification from at least one other source.

Readers' questions and comments are welcome.

Contact the author at:

joemarconi@sbcglobal.net.

Best Web sites for Writers

Sharp Writer

http://www.johntcullen.com/sharpwriter/

Preditors & Editors

http://www.anotherealm.com/prededitors/

Fiction Fundamentals

http://home.earthlink.net/~tgshaw/index.html

Recommended Reading

Several times throughout this book, it was noted that what most writers have in common is that they love to read. There are many very good books on writing or for writers or simply excellent books for writers to read. These are, in the opinion of this author, among the very best:

The War Against Cliché. Martin Amis (Miramax, 2001)

The Copy Workshop Workbook. Bruce Bendinger (The Copy Workshop, 2002)

For Writers Only. Sophy Burnham (Random House, 1996)

A Heartbreaking Work of Staggering Genius. Dave Eggers (Simon & Schuster, 2000)

The Book of Gossage. Howard Luck Gossage (The Copy Workshop, 2006)

On Writing: A Memoir of the Craft. Stephen King (Scribner, 2000)

The Forest for the Trees. Betsy Lerner (Riverhead Trade, 2001)

Consciousness and the Novel. David Lodge (Harvard University Press, 2002)

The Practice of Writing. David Lodge (Viking, 1996)

The Elements of Style. William Strunk, Jr., E.B. White (Kt Publishing, 2004)

A Writer's Life. Gay Talese (Knopf, 2006)

Word Court. Barbara Wallraff (Harvest/HBJ, 2001)

On Writing Well. William Zinsser (HarperPerennial, 1998)